Management Science - Theory and Applications

Business Issues, Competition and Entrepreneurship

nova
science publishers
www.novapublishers.com

Management Science - Theory and Applications

Special Human Resource Management Practices and Strategy
Ömer Yazıcı, PhD (Editor)
2022. ISBN: 978-1-68507-279-7 (Hardcover)
2022. ISBN: 978-1-68507-518-7 (eBook)

Emotional Intelligence and the Leader's Role
Cam Caldwell, PhD and Verl Anderson, PhD (Authors)
2021. ISBN: 978-1-68507-004-5 (Hardcover)
2021. ISBN: 978-1-68507-065-6 (eBook)

Employee Engagement: A Human Resource Management Perspective
Cam Caldwell, PhD and Verl Anderson, PhD (Authors)
2021. ISBN: 978-1-53619-687-0 (Hardcover)
2021. ISBN: 978-1-53619-735-8 (eBook)

Emerging Human and Techno-Human Business Management Dynamics in a Globalized Environment
Christina Koutra, PhD and Hafiz Imtiaz Ahmad (Editors)
2020. ISBN: 978-1-53618-602-4 (Hardcover)
2020. ISBN: 978-1-53618-667-3 (eBook)

Wellness Management for Educators and Entrepreneurs
Joosung J. Lee and Jungeun Kim (Authors)
2020. ISBN: 978-1-53618-534-8 (eBook)

More information about this series can be found at https://novapublishers.com/shop/employee-engagement-a-human-resource-management-perspective/

Cam Caldwell and Verl Anderson

Leading with Passion

nova
science publishers
www.novapublishers.com

https://doi.org/10.52305/OFUS5291

NOTICE TO THE READER

Library of Congress Cataloging-in-Publication Data

ISBN: 978-1-68507-007-6

Published by Nova Science Publishers, Inc. † New York

Contents

Preface

Leading others requires the ability to touch hearts as well as minds. That ability involves a leader's understanding of what matters to others and the capacity to inspire and motivate. The emotional connection of leaders with those whom they lead is an important part of the leader's relationship with colleagues.

This book addresses the nature of passion and emotion as a part of the leader-follower relationship. Those who lead must establish the ability to understand others' hopes, desires, and emotional priorities in order to unlock their highest potential. Great organizations and effective leaders accomplish extraordinary results by obtaining the commitment and dedication of all of their members.

Leading with passion means that a leader also understands her or his own motivations and develops the ability to use those feelings and emotions in healthy and constructive ways. Passion enriches and enlarges the capacity to feel strongly and to care completely. But passion must also be fully understood and regulated in appropriate ways for a leader to be most effective.

We trust that those who read this book will enjoy its chapters and will contemplate the ideas, suggestions, and challenges contained herein. We encourage the readers to utilize their passions to live a fuller and more satisfying life themselves – and to use those same passions to bless and serve the lives of others.

Cam Caldwell, PhD
Verl Anderson, PhD

November 2021

Chapter 1

Leading with Passion – What It Means and Why It Matters

In writing about the importance of passion, Nelson Mandela once said, "There is no passion to be found playing small – in settling for a life that is less than the one you are capable of living.[1]" Playing small, or making an effort that is incomplete or that demonstrates a half-hearted regard for a goal to be achieved fails to earn the respect, commitment, and followership of others.

For leaders, living a life that seeks to fulfill one's highest potential is rarely achieved without a passionate commitment to high ideals and a worthy purpose.

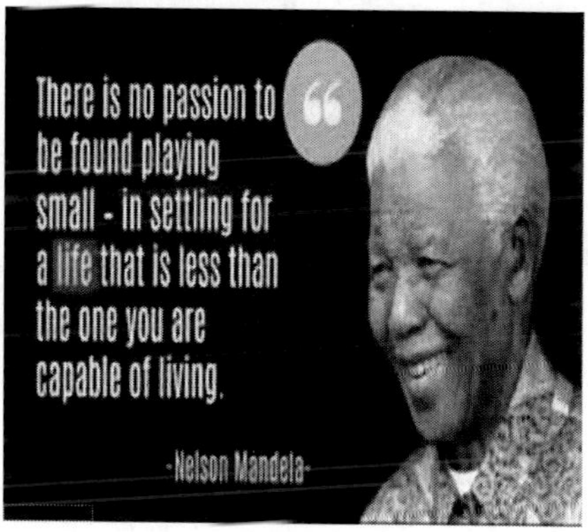

For leaders, living a life that seeks to fulfill one's highest potential is rarely achieved without a passionate commitment to high ideals and a worthy purpose. In a world where trust in leaders is often lacking[2], people crave leaders who are good, worthy of being followed, and uncompromising in their commitment to excellence[3].

---

[1] Nelson Mandela Quotes. (n.d.). BrainyQuote.com. Found on May 13, 2021at https://www.brainyquote.com/quotes/nelson_mandela_391070.

[2] Harrington, M., (2017). Survey: People's Trust has Declined in Business, Media, Government, and NGOs." *Harvard Business Review*, January 16, 2017 and found online on May 13, 2021 at https://hbr.org/2017/01/survey-peoples-trust-has-declined-in-business-media-government-and-ngo,

[3] Andersen, E. (2012). *Leading So People Will Follow*. San Francisco, CA: Jossey-Bass, p. 1.

The purpose of this book is to identify the importance of leading with passion – the ability to bring light into a world of uncertainty and inspire others to cast off fears, overcome doubts, and the self-limiting beliefs that impede the achieving of great potential[4]. The role of this first chapter is to introduce the importance of leading with passion and to identify ten defining qualities associated with passion. We begin by first defining passion and briefly explaining how each of the ten qualities contributes to effective leadership. We follow that introduction with a summary of the remaining chapters of this book and conclude with encouragement to the reader to incorporate passion as (s)he seeks to become a more effective leader and a source of inspiration for others.

> The **purpose of this book** is to **identify the importance of leading with passion** – the **ability to bring light into a world of uncertainty** and **inspire others to cast off fears, overcome doubts,** and the **self-limiting beliefs** that **impede the achieving of great potential.**

Defining Passion

Most often passions are viewed by individuals as emotional states However, Robert Solomon, argued that emotions are actually highly rational – although they clearly include an affective emotional response as well[5]. We concur with Solomon's logic and cite the Theory of Reasoned Action in explaining how passion incorporates both the cognitive and affective elements of human

---

[4] Murphy, J. J., (2010). *Leading with Passion: 10 Essentials for Inspiring Others*. Naperville, IL: Simple Truths Publishing.

[5] Solomon, R. C., (2003). "Emotions, Thoughts, and Feelings: "What is a 'Cognitive Theory' of the Emotions and Does It Neglect Affectivity?" *Royal Institute of Philosophy Supplement*, Vol. 52, pp. 1-18.

decision making[6]. Figure 1, provided here, identifies the link between the cognitive and affective elements associated with human behavior.

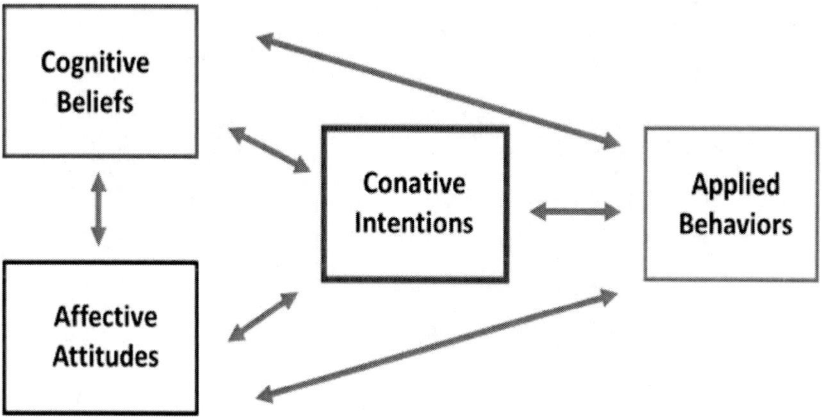

Figure 1. The Theory of Reasoned Action.

As the Theory of Reasoned Action suggests, cognitive beliefs and affective attitudes and emotions are constantly interacting and impact both intentions and behaviors[7]. As Solomon suggests, passions of all types are affected by rational thought and affective emotions[8]. Often emotions can hijack rational thinking, but by incorporating the self-awareness and self-management of Emotional Intelligence individuals may manage both the cognitive and the affective elements of decision-making in the productive application of passionate commitment[9].

Passions are expressed in a broad array of ways. Passion can be directed toward another person, such as in the expression of deep regard or love for a friend. Passions also play a major role in the pursuit of a valued purpose or a noble objective that motivates a life. As an expression of personal devotion, passion may also be expressed as a deep commitment to an institution, a faith, or a divine power.

---

[6] Fishbein, M & Ajzen, I., (2011). *Predicting and Changing Behavior: The Reasoned Action Approach*. East Sussex, UK: Psychology Press.
[7] *Ibid.*
[8] Solomon, (2003), op. cit.
[9] Goleman, D., (2005). *Emotional Intelligence: Why It Can Matter More Than IQ*. New York: Bantam Publishing.

Emotions can **hijack rational thinking,** but by **incorporating the self-awareness and self-management** of Emotional Intelligence **individuals may effectively manage** both **the cognitive and the affective elements of decision-making** in the **productive application of passionate commitment**.

Passion can also convey frustration, disappointment, and anger and can result in negative outcomes when emotions are inappropriate to a situation or context. In whatever ways they are expressed or manifest, passion conveys a depth of intensity that drives an individual to take actions that reflect what (s)he deeply seeks to communicate or accomplish.

Passion conveys a **depth of intensity** that **drives an individual** to **take actions that reflect** what (s)he deeply **seeks to communicate or accomplish.**

Based upon the current research, we have identified ten qualities that provide insights into the importance of leading with passion. Each of those qualities will be discussed throughout the chapters that follow in substantially greater detail, but the summaries provided below offer an introductory insight into each of those ten qualities.

Purpose

Purpose is the underlying reason which defines why people act as they do. Having a commitment to a specific purpose enables a person to be constantly motivated, even when seemingly overwhelming hardships must be faced[10]. Purpose is the yardstick for measuring one's success and is the driving force that becomes the deep reason for a person's existence[11]. Purpose provides direction for passion and is the "why" that guides passion in leadership.

Purpose provides direction for passion **and is the "why"** that **guides passion in leadership.**

Resilience

Resilience is the capacity to deal with whatever life throws at you[12]. Life contains its bumps and roadblocks and resilience in dealing with set-backs is best driven by the passion to succeed, despite life's many obstacles. Viewing obstacles as both challenges and opportunities to learn is possible when leaders focus on goals that they are striving to achieve and the importance of achieving valued outcomes[13].

---

[10] Frankl, V., (1988). *Man's Search for Meaning*. New York: Pocket Books.

[11] Ho, L. (2020). "How to Connect Passion and Purpose for Fulfillment in Life." Lifehack, July 17, 2020 and found online on May 15, 2021 at How To Connect Passion and Purpose For Fulfillment In Life (lifehack.org).

[12] Pennock, S. F., (2020). "Resilience in Positive Psychology: Bouncing Back and Staying Strong." *Positive Psychology*, December 10, 2020 and found online on May 15, 2021 at Resilience in Positive Psychology: Bouncing Back & Staying Strong.

[13] *Ibid*.

Life contains its bumps and road blocks and **resilience in dealing with struggles** and set-backs is **best driven by the passion to succeed,** despite life's **many obstacles.**

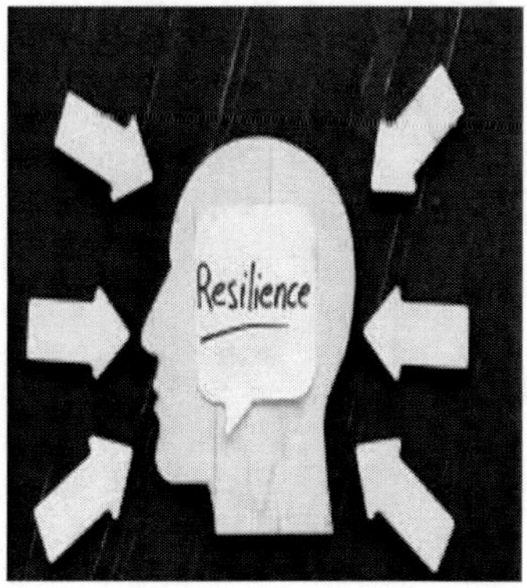

Perseverance

Perseverance is the ability to carry on one's efforts without giving up, despite whatever obstacles must be faced[14]. Perseverance is often associated with a constant effort to learn and to master a task and is associated with a sustained interest in the pursuit of goals by constant effort.[15] Leaders show their perseverance by their fierce resolve to improve and to exemplify what they believe to be important[16].

Leaders **show their perseverance** by their **fierce resolve to improve** and to **exemplify** what they **believe to be important.**

[14] Mirsirlisoy, E. (2018). "It's Not All Perseverance, You Need Passion Too." December 8, 2018 and found online on May 15, 2021 at Grit? It's Not All Perseverance, You Need Passion Too | by Erman Misirlisoy, PhD | Medium.

[15] Duckworth, A., (2018). *GRIT: The Power of Passion and Persistence*. London, UK: Vermilion Publishing.

[16] Collins, J., (2001). *Good to Great: Why Some Companies Make the Leap . . . . And Others Don't*. New York: HarperCollins.

Self-Confidence

Self-confidence contributes to passion in leaders by reinforcing their optimism about what they can accomplish to ultimately achieve their goals. Despite the challenges and inevitable disappointments that may occur, self-confidence enables leaders to keep working and stay committed. Self-confidence is a reflection of the authentic self that sees past imperfections and recognizes one's highest potential[17] - making it possible to remain positive in a "trial and error" world[18].

Self-confidence is a **reflection of the authentic self** that **sees past imperfections** and **recognizes one's highest potential**-- making it **possible to remain positive** in a **"trial and error" world.**

Effort

Effort is the hard work, the attention to detail, the following through, and the diligence in the pursuit of a goal that enables a leader to set the example for others. Passion is measured by the effort that an individual makes to achieve that which (s)he is committed to achieving or seeks to accomplish. Constant effort that demonstrates a leader's fierce resolve to succeed captures the attention of others and earns their respect and followership[19].

---

[17] Davenport, B., (2017). "How Seeking Your Passion Boosts Self-Esteem." Huff Post, December 6, 2017 and found online on May 15, 2021 at How Seeking Your Passion Boosts Self-Esteem | HuffPost Life.

[18] Rubin, J., (2016). "Self Confidence and Finding Your Life Passion." Lost Highway Blues, July 15, 2016 and found online on May 15, 2021 at Self-confidence and Finding Your Life Passion (janerubinphd.com).

[19] Collins, (2001), *op.cit.*

Passion is **measured by the effort** that an individual makes **to achieve that which (s)he is committed** to achieving or **seeks to accomplish.**

Success is dependent on effort.

Sophocles

Trust

Trust is the relinquishing of one's personal will to another person or to a worthy ideal in the pursuit of a sought-after goal – expecting that a highly-desired positive outcome will ultimately result[20]. Trust in relationships is the glue that holds organizations together. A leader's willingness to commit herself/himself in conditions of uncertainty reflects the belief that the outcome to be achieved is worth the personal investment[21].

Trust is **the relinquishing of one's personal will**to **another person** or to a **worthy ideal** in the **pursuit of a sought-after goal** -- **expecting that a highly-desired positive outcome** will **ultimately result.**

Trust is Action

---

[20] Caldwell, C. & Anderson, V., (2019). "Trust from a Transformative Perspective" in *Trust, Trustworthiness, and Stewardship: A Transformative Approach*. C. Caldwell & V. Anderson (Eds.) .Hauppauge, New York: NOVA Publishing, Chapter 3.

[21] Mayer, R. C., Davis, J. H. & Schoorman, F. D., (1995). "An Integrative Model of Organizational Trust." *Academy of Management Review*, Vol. 20, No. 3, pp. 709-734.

Hope

Hope is an expectant desire that views the world optimistically and with an expectation that good will ultimately prevail when individuals put forth their best efforts. Implicit in hope is the integration of planning, motivation, and determination[22]. Hope involves personal courage coupled with a positive belief in the possibilities that exist in life[23]. Hope anticipates possibilities that others who are pessimistic fail to envision, and it is the leader's hopeful vision that inspires others[24].

Hope involves **personal courage** coupled with a **positive belief** in the **possibilities that exist** in life.

Hope
IS PASSION
FOR WHAT IS
POSSIBLE

Enthusiasm

Enthusiasm is the intense degree of enjoyment, interest, or approval that is expressed by an individual and reflects an individual's personal feelings associated with a situation or event. Derived from the early Greek, enthusiasm literally means "God within you" and is sometimes referred to as "divine energy" associated with the pursuing of a personal dream or goal[25]. Leaders encourage the hearts of others by the optimistic enthusiasm which they exhibit – coupled with the acumen to make dreams become realities[26].

---

[22] Maholmes, V., (2014). *Fostering Resilience and Well-Being in Children and Families in Poverty: Why Hope Still Matters*. Oxford, UK: Oxford University Press.

[23] *Ibid*.

[24] Kouzes, J. M. & Posner, B.Z., (2017). *The Leadership Challenge: How to Make Extraordinary Things Happen in Organizations* (7th ed.). San Francisco, CA: Jossey-Bass, pp. 93-142.

[25] Van Lint, I., (2021). "Characteristics of Successful People." Enthusiasm found online on May 15, 2021at Enthusiasm is passion. Enthusiasm is living your dream. - Enthusiasm - Ineke Van Lint (enthousiasme.info).

[26] Kouzes & Posner, (2017), op. cit., pp. 245-294.

Leaders **encourage the hearts** of others **by the optimistic enthusiasm** which **they exhibit – coupled with the acumen to make dreams become realities.**

Humility

Humility combines 1) a clear knowledge of oneself, 2) an appreciation for the importance of others, and 3) an inspired commitment to constantly improve based upon those realizations[27]. As the recognition and acknowledgement of one's "divine indebtedness" to become the best person that one can be, humility drives individuals to transcend their previous best efforts in the pursuit of the good[28]. Leaders with humility accept responsibility for the shortcomings of organizations while giving credit to others for successes[29].

As the **recognition and acknowledgement** of one's **"divine indebtedness" to become the best person that one can be,** humility **drives individuals to transcend their previous best efforts** in the **pursuit of the good.**

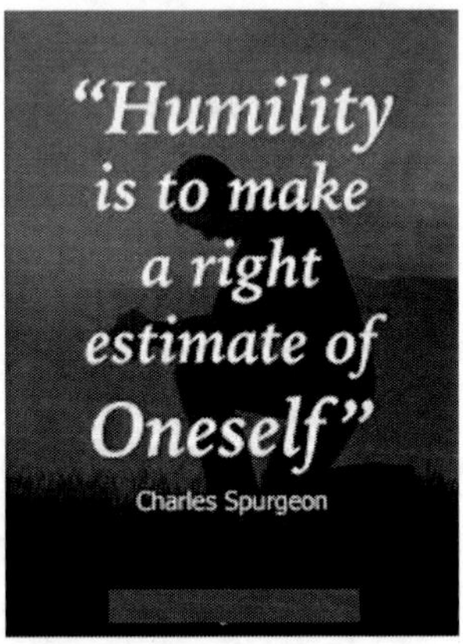

[27] Owens, B. P. & Hekman, D. R., (2016). "How Does Leader Humility Affect Team Performance? Exploring the Mechanisms of Contagion and Collective Promotion Focus." *Academy of Management Journal*, Vol. 59, No. 3, pp. 787-818.

[28] Browning, R. M., (2005). *Resolving Concerns.* Atlanta, GA: Self-published.

[29] Collins, (2001), *op. cit.*

Caring

Caring is a fundamental moral virtue[30] and the essence of love[31]. Caring about others and their growth demonstrates the authentic and genuine valuing of others that cannot be faked. Caring acknowledges the close relationship between the parties and the concern for others' best interests[32]. Leaders who love their employees demonstrate a commitment to their welfare, growth, and wholeness and honor those employees in so doing[33].

Caring is a fundamental moral virtue and the essence of love.

Caring

Each of these ten qualities is associated with leading with passion and a leader's ability to inspire and motivate others. All ten of these qualities are addressed in much greater detail throughout this book. Throughout these chapters, we define passion as *an intense and powerful feeling of commitment, compelling desire, and enthusiasm directed toward a purpose, institution, person, or objective*. Without passion, those who live inevitably fail to win the hearts and minds of those who they seek to engage and motivate[34]. Leading with passion enables leaders to create commitment that goes far beyond their own efforts – a vital trait that the current research about leadership affirms that so many modern leaders desperately need to develop[35].

---

[30] Gilligan, C., (2016). *In a Different Voice: Psychological Theory and Women's Development*. Boston, MA: Harvard University Press.

[31] Fromm, E., (2006). *The Art of Loving*. New York: Harper Perennial.

[32] Gilligan, (2016), *op. cit.*

[33] Caldwell, C. & Anderson, V., (Eds.) (2019). "Love and Trust: The Leader's Gifts" in *Leading with Love*, C. Caldwell, C. & V. Anderson, V., (Eds.): Hauppauge, New York: NOVA Publishing, Chapter 10.

[34] Kouzes, J. M. & Posner, B. Z., (2003). *Encouraging the Heart: A Leader's Guide to Rewarding and Recognizing Others*. San Francisco, CA: Jossey-Bass.

[35] Clifton, J. & Harter, J., (2019). *It's the Manager*. Omaha, NE: Gallup Press.

We define passion as *an intense and powerful feeling of commitment, compelling desire, and enthusiasm directed toward a purpose, institution, person, or objective*.

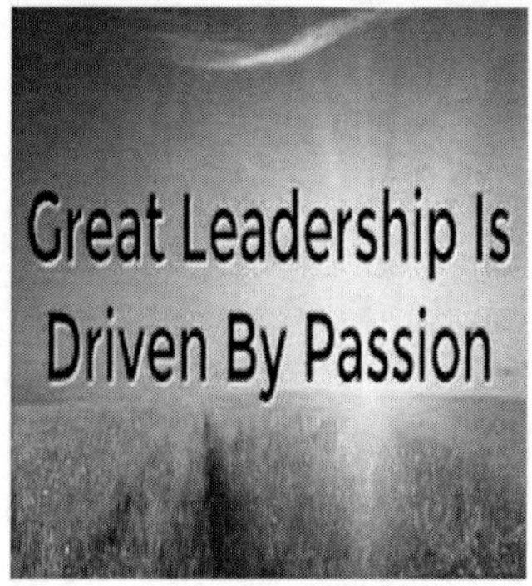

Summary of Remaining Chapters

Each of the chapters that follow in this book have been written to help individuals to understand how the qualities of passion enable leaders to establish connection with the members of their organizations. We recognize that each reader may have different interests and priorities related to leading with passion. For that reason, we briefly summarize the contents of each of these chapters – but ask the reader to also be willing to explore other elements of leading with passion that (s)he may not have previously considered to be as significant. Respectfully, we suggest that each of the remaining chapters offers insights that can enlighten leaders about how they are perceived by those whom they lead and serve.

Chapter 2 – Leading with Passion in an Arms-length World

The focus of this chapter is on the importance of leaders restoring employee commitment and trust by leading with passion. We begin the chapter by describing the arms-length approach to employee relationships that characterizes many modern leaders and explain eight underlying assumptions implicit in arm's-length relationships with employees. We contrast this leadership approach by identifying five key factors that are critical for leading with passion, personal dedication, and fierce resolve. Following that summary, we present ten recommendations for leaders to consider to regain the employee trust and commitment that has undermined employee engagement. The chapter concludes with an invitation to leaders to rethink their assumptions about their relationships with employees.

Chapter 3 – Leading with Commitment

The purpose of this chapter is to examine the nature of commitment and the factors upon which it is based. We begin the chapter by defining the nature of commitment and identifying its importance as a characteristic of effective leaders. We identify ten reasons why commitments are not always honored and explain why keeping commitments is often difficult. We then identify six antecedents to commitment and describe how those antecedents influence the willingness and ability to sustain individual effort in the pursuit of an intended goal. We include in that assessment the role of commitment in reflecting the individual identity of an individual and the strength of the values that are the underlying factors that determine action. We close the chapter with encouragement to leaders to understand that to which they are committed and to appreciate the impact of their choices on their ability to lead effectively.

Chapter 4 – Passion, Humility, and Fierce Resolve

The focus of this chapter is on the importance of understanding the nature of humility as a quality that motivates leaders to achieve not only outstanding results but constant and continuous improvement in partnership with others. The chapter begins by defining humility as a leadership perspective that incorporates great commitment and a passion for excellence. The chapter offers ten recommendations for leaders as they interact with others and concludes with a challenge to leaders to incorporate humility in their relationships.

Chapter 5 – Persistence, Perseverance, and Character

This power of integrity is based upon each person's persistence, perseverance, and character – the focus upon which this chapter is based. We begin this chapter by distinguishing the differences between persistence and perseverance and their relationship to personal character. Following that introduction, we examine seven characteristics that lead to perseverance and that contribute to a leader's ability to demonstrate her/his personal character and integrity. The chapter concludes with a challenge to leaders to understand the importance of persevering as they strive to earn the followership and commitment of others.

Chapter 6 – Serving with Passion

We begin the chapter by describing the nature of servant leadership and explaining seven fundamental pillars upon which servant leadership is based. We then identify eight important ways that the servant leader perspective establishes better relationships and builds more effective organizations. The chapter concludes with a challenge to leaders to incorporate servant leadership in honoring their responsibilities to their organizations and to those with whom they work.

Chapter 7 – Hope as a Form of Passion

The purpose of this chapter is to provide insights about the nature of hope as a resource to leaders. Although hope may be an elusive concept, it nonetheless has been the motivation for human effort and positive expectations for millennia. We begin the chapter by defining hope as it applies in individual lives. We identify seven attributes of hope that refine its definition in the practical world. We then suggest five positive qualities of hope that are assets to leadership but also identify how relying on hope can be dysfunctional for leaders and organizations when hope is not viewed realistically. The chapter concludes by encouraging leaders to understand the nature and limits of hope.

Chapter 8 – Enthusiasm as Effective Leadership

The purpose of this chapter is to define enthusiasm and identify why enthusiasm is so vital in the relationship between leaders and those whom they serve. We explain why enthusiasm plays an important role in motivating performance and in empowering those who possess it. We identify five ways that leaders can increase enthusiasm within their organizations and encourage leaders to consider the benefits of being personally enthusiastic in their relationships with others as they strive to increase their effectiveness.

Chapter 9 – Ethical Stewardship as Quiet Passion

The focus of this chapter is on the role of ethical stewards who quietly but passionately lead organizations as they assist those with whom they labor to achieve the highest possible potential for their organizations. We begin the chapter by explaining stewardship theory and differentiate it from agency and stakeholder theories. We describe the unique strengths of ethical stewardship as a leadership model and identify eight principles upon which ethical stewardship is based. We conclude the chapter by encouraging those who lead to adopt the principles of ethical stewardship as they work within their organizations.

Chapter 10 – Leading with Passion and Self-Control

The purpose of this chapter is to identify the complex nature of passion as an inspiring quality of leaders but to also emphasize the importance of passion that positively contributes to an individual's life, growth, and effectiveness with others. We begin the chapter by defining passion as a motivational force that drives individuals in the pursuit of a desired objective. We distinguish between obsessive and harmonious passion and note that passion can have positive and negative implications for individuals. We explain the relationship between passion and the individual identity and offer six suggestions for leaders to help them to assess the ways in which they monitor themselves, and control their emotions as they express their passion in the leadership role. The chapter concludes with a challenge to leaders to apply these suggestions as they integrate passion and self-control in interacting with others.

Incorporating Passion

There is rarely any "instant pudding" approach to changing individual lives or building relationships with others[36]. The introspection required to incorporate the many and diverse qualities associated with leading with passion demands that leaders invest in understanding themselves and the ten qualities that are described within these pages.

Leading with passion requires a complex combination of ethical, interpersonal, and organizational attributes and insights that somehow **have eluded the perceptions of many modern leaders.**

Leading with passion requires a complex combination of ethical, interpersonal, and organizational attributes and insights that somehow have eluded the perceptions of many modern leaders. The challenge to leaders is to recognize that all of the qualities described within this book are essential for them to be perceived as personally credible – in addition to a combination of technical skills and capabilities that are required in every business endeavor.

We encourage readers to open their minds to the importance of all ten of the qualities that are part of leading with passion and to take the time to conduct a personal inventory of each quality – including seeking feedback from those with whom they labor to identify how others also perceive how well they are doing in incorporating the qualities within leadership relationships. We quickly acknowledge that the quest to become a more effective leader may take constant effort over an extended period of time – but we promise that the commitment to leading with passion will ultimately bear fruit.

---

[36] Deming, W. E., (2000). *Out of the Crisis*. Cambridge, MA: MIT Press.

The quest to become a more effective leader may take **constant effort over an extended period of time** – but we **promise that the commitment** to leading **with passion** will **ultimately bear fruit.**

We affirm that, as Nelson Mandela has suggested, "settling for a life that is less than the one you are capable of living" is a choice that ultimately leads to regret and disappointment. Leading with passion has the potential capability to make life more satisfying, more meaningful, more productive, and more personally and professionally rewarding.

References

Andersen, E. (2012). *Leading So People Will Follow*. San Francisco, CA: Jossey-Bass, p. 1.

Browning, R. M., (2005). *Resolving Concerns*. Atlanta, GA: Self-published.

Caldwell, C. & Anderson, V., (Eds.) (2019). "Love and Trust: The Leader's Gifts" in *Leading with Love*, C. Caldwell, C. & V. Anderson, V., (Eds.): Hauppauge, New York: NOVA Publishing, Chapter 10.

Caldwell, C. & Anderson, V., (2019). "Trust from a Transformative Perspective" in *Trust, Trustworthiness, and Stewardship: A Transformative Approach*. C. Caldwell & V. Anderson (Eds.) .Hauppauge, New York: NOVA Publishing, Chapter 3.

Clifton, J. & Harter, J., (2019). *It's the Manager*. Omaha, NE: Gallup Press.

Collins, J., (2001). *Good to Great: Why Some Companies Make the Leap . . . . And Others Don't*. New York: HarperCollins.

Davenport, B., (2017). "How Seeking Your Passion Boosts Self-Esteem." Huff Post, December 6, 2017 and found online on May 15, 2021 at How Seeking Your Passion Boosts Self-Esteem | HuffPost Life.

Deming, W. E., (2000). *Out of the Crisis*. Cambridge, MA: MIT Press.

Duckworth, A., (2018). *GRIT: The Power of Passion and Persistence*. London, UK: Vermilion Publishing.

Fishbein, M & Ajzen, I., (2011). *Predicting and Changing Behavior: The Reasoned Action Approach*. East Sussex, UK: Psychology Press.

Frankl, V., (1988). *Man's Search for Meaning*. New York: Pocket Books.

Gilligan, C., (2016). *In a Different Voice: Psychological Theory and Women's Development*. Boston, MA: Harvard University Press.

Goleman, D., (2005). *Emotional Intelligence: Why It Can Matter More Than IQ*. New York: Bantam Publishing.

Harrington, M., (2017). Survey: People's Trust has Declined in Business, Media, Government, and NGOs." *Harvard Business Review*, January 16, 2017 and found online on May 13, 2021 at https://hbr.org/2017/01/survey-peoples-trust-has-declined-in-business-media-government-and-ngo,

Ho, L. (2020). "How to Connect Passion and Purpose for Fulfillment in Life." Lifehack, July 17, 2020 and found online on May 15, 2021 at How To Connect Passion and Purpose For Fulfillment In Life (lifehack.org).

Kouzes, J. M. & Posner, B. Z., (2017). *The Leadership Challenge: How to Make Extraordinary Things Happen in Organizations* (7th ed.). San Francisco, CA: Jossey-Bass, pp. 93-142.

Kouzes, J. M. & Posner, B. Z., (2003). *Encouraging the Heart: A Leader's Guide to Rewarding and Recognizing Others*. San Francisco, CA: Jossey-Bass.

Maholmes, V., (2014). *Fostering Resilience and Well-Being in Children and Families in Poverty: Why Hope Still Matters*. Oxford, UK: Oxford University Press.

Mayer, R. C., Davis, J. H. & Schoorman, F. D., (1995). "An Integrative Model of Organizational Trust." *Academy of Management Review*, Vol. 20, No. 3, pp. 709-734.

Mirsirlisoy, E. (2018). "It's Not All Perseverance, You Need Passion Too." December 8, 2018 and found online on May 15, 2021 at Grit? It's Not All Perseverance, You Need Passion Too | by Erman Misirlisoy, PhD | Medium.

Murphy, J. J., (2010). *Leading with Passion: 10 Essentials for Inspiring Others*. Naperville, IL: Simple Truths Publishing.

Nelson Mandela Quotes. (n.d.). BrainyQuote.com. Found on May 13, 2021at https://www.brainyquote.com/quotes/nelson_mandela_391070.

Owens, B. P. & Hekman, D. R., (2016). "How Does Leader Humility Affect Team Performance? Exploring the Mechanisms of Contagion and Collective Promotion Focus." *Academy of Management Journal*, Vol. 59, No. 3, pp. 787-818.

Pennock, S. F., (2020). "Resilience in Positive Psychology: Bouncing Back and Staying Strong." *Positive Psychology*, December 10, 2020 and found online on May 15, 2021 at Resilience in Positive Psychology: Bouncing Back & Staying Strong.

Rubin, J., (2016). "Self Confidence and Finding Your Life Passion." Lost Highway Blues, July 15, 2016 and found online on May 15, 2021 at Self-confidence and Finding Your Life Passion (janerubinphd.com) Solomon, R. C., (2003). "Emotions, Thoughts, and Feelings: "What is a 'Cognitive Theory' of the Emotions and Does It Neglect Affectivity?" *Royal Institute of Philosophy Supplement*, Vol. 52, pp. 1-18.

Van Lint, I., (2021). "Characteristics of Successful People." Enthusiasm found online on May 15, 2021at Enthusiasm is passion. Enthusiasm is living your dream. - Enthusiasm - Ineke Van Lint (enthousiasme.info).

Chapter 2

Leading with Passion in an Arms-Length World

The workplace culture has been greatly affected by a world financial crisis, the "work from home" requirements of COVID-19, and the expanded hiring of part-time employees. Stanford University's Jeffrey Pfeffer expressed concern about the deterioration of the employment contract between leaders and employees more than two decades ago[37]. The "arms-length" approach that typifies the modern working world has resulted in reduced employee engagement[38], decreased trust in leaders and organizations[39], and increased concerns about the sustainability of companies in today's highly-competitive global environment[40].

> The **"arms-length" approach that typifies the modern working world** has resulted in **reduced employee engagement, decreased trust in leaders** and organizations, and **increased concerns** about the **sustainability of companies** in **today's highly-competitive global environment.**

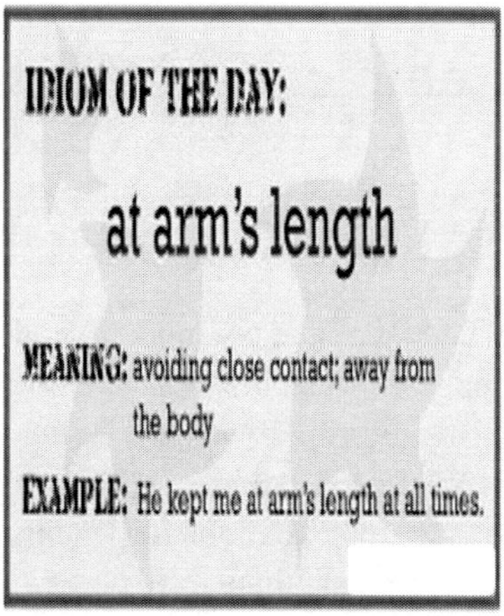

---

[37] Pfeffer, J., (1998). *The Human Equation: Building Profits by Putting People First*. Boston, MA: Harvard Business Review Press.

[38] Clifton, J. & Harter, J., (2019). *It's the Manager*. Omaha, NE: Gallup Press.

[39] Edelman, (2021). "Edelman Trust Barometer 2021." Found online on July 4, 2021 at 2021 Edelman Trust Barometer | Edelman.

[40] Maudlin, J., (2021). "4 Economic Challenges for 2021." *Forbes*, January 18, 2021 and found online on July 4, 2021 at 4 Economic Challenges For 2021 (forbes.com).

The growing evidence about leadership in the modern organization is that organizations are struggling to motivate their employees, retain employee commitment, and sustain their loyalty[41]. According to a 2017 study conducted by Mental Health America, the workplace is a source of increasing employee dissatisfaction and employee depression[42]. Employees complain of workplace stress and isolation and the study reported the alarming finding that 70 percent of workers say that they were actively looking for a new job[43].

According to **a 2017 study** conducted by Mental Health America, the **workplace is a source of increasing employee dissatisfaction** and employee **depression**.

The focus of this chapter is on the importance of leaders restoring employee commitment and trust by leading with passion. We begin the chapter by describing the arms-length approach to employee relationships that has characterized many modern leaders and explain eight underlying assumptions implicit in relationships with employees. We contrast this leadership approach by identifying five key factors that are critical for leading with passion, personal dedication, and fierce resolve. Following that summary, we present ten recommendations for leaders to consider to regain the employee trust and commitment that has undermined employee engagement. The chapter concludes with an invitation to leaders to rethink their assumptions about their relationships with employees.

---

[41] Clifton & Harter, (2019), *op. cit.*

[42] Hellebuyck, M., Nguyen, T. Halphern, M., Fritze, D. & Kennedy, J., (2017). *Mind the Workplace*. Lancaster, CA: Mental Health America.

[43] Schwantes, M., (2018). "A New Study Reveals 70 Percent of Workers Say They Are Actively Looking for a New Job. Here's the Reason in Five Words." Inc., December 4. 2018 and found online on July 4, 2021 at A New Study Reveals 70 Percent of Workers Say They Are Actively Looking for a New Job. Here's the Reason in 5 Words | Inc.com.

Arms-Length Relationships

The world in which many employees work is characterized by a formalized exchange of wages for hours worked – with employees treated as performers of a restricted set of tasks with specifically defined responsibilities and outcomes. The nature of the employer-employee relationship is often simply transactional and often does not acknowledge either the individual needs or the capabilities of employees[44]. The consequences of hiring employees for part-time positions and treating people as commodities often results in those employees feeling taken advantage of and reluctant to give their best efforts to their employer – creating lose-lose outcomes for the company and the persons hired[45].

The consequences of **hiring employees for part-time positions** and **treating people as commodities** often results in those **employees feeling taken advantage** of and **reluctant to give their best efforts to their employer** – creating **lose-lose outcomes** for **the company and the persons hired**.

Jean Murray defined an arms-length transaction as "a transaction is one in which both parties are acting in their own best interest. That means they have negotiated fairly on price, and neither party is giving the other one a deal better or worse than the market would dictate because of an existing relationship between them[46]." The assumption between the parties in an arms-length relationship is that the goals for both parties are purely economic and self-

[44] Burns, J. M., (2010). *Leadership*. New York: Harper Perennial.

[45] Caldwell, C., Floyd, L. A., Taylor, J. & Woodard, B. (2014). "Beneficence as a Source of Competitive Advantage." *Journal of Management Development*, Vol. 33, Iss. 10, pp. 1057-1069.

[46] Murray, J., (2020). "What is an Arms Length Transaction?" *the balance small business*, October 30, 2020 and found online on July 5, 2021 at An Arm's Length Transaction: What Is It? (thebalancesmb.com).

serving, rather than mutually beneficial and collaborative. This transactional approach has been largely adopted by employers who have treated employees almost entirely as task performers.

The **mental model in an arms-length relationship** is that the **goals for both parties are purely economic and self-serving,** rather than **mutually beneficial and collaborative.** This **transactional approach** has been **largely adopted by employers** who have **treated employees almost entirely as task performers.**

Leadership expert, James MacGregor Burns explained that the transactional approach focused on employee compliance with an employer's standards and essentially viewed employees as being owed little more than "a fair day's pay for a fair day's work[47]." This approach is decidedly one-sided in which managers and supervisors make decisions and create relationships where employees are told to leave their brains at the door – often feeling that they are not really treated as full partners in the work relationship[48].

The consequence of employees being treated as "Its" rather than as "Yous" has had a measurable impact on employee attitudes. More than half of all employees in a Harvard University study expressed little trust in their supervisors and reported that they would rather trust a complete stranger than their boss[49]. Increasingly, employers demonstrate that they feel little obligation to their employees' long-term best interests – best evidenced by the

---

[47] Burns, J. M., (2010). Leadership.

[48] Pfeffer, (1998), *op. cit.*

[49] Sturt & Nordstrom, (2018). "10 Shocking Workplace Stats You Need to Know." Forbes, March 8, 2018 and found online on September 30, 2020 at https://www.forbes.com/sites/davidsturt/2018/03/08/10-shocking-workplace-stats-you-need-to-know/#2a90c892f3af.

fact that the full-time job with benefits, insurance, and sick leave is quickly becoming a thing of the past[50].

More than half of all employees in a **Harvard University study** expressed **little trust in their supervisors** and reported that **they would rather trust a complete stranger** than their boss.

The "gig economy," in which temporary and part-time jobs are referred to as "gigs," has resulted in a huge number of individuals feeling disenchanted about their futures and concerned about their long-term ability to provide for themselves and their families. According to a study by the University of New Hampshire's Rebecca Glauber, one in four part-time employees actually qualified as a person living in poverty and was unable to provide adequately for themselves and their families[51].

This arms-length treatment of employees typically reflects a corporation's concern for short term profit taking and cost cutting, rather than pursuing the creation of long-term value for a firm and for customers[52]. Rather than seeking to build organizations around a culture of high trust and employee empowerment, companies have chosen instead to focus on a relationship with employees that mirrors the transactional exchange of dollars paid for tasks performed – often with little concern for the implications of that approach on both their employees and their long-term competitive position[53].

The assumptions about the arms-length treatment of employees reflect a number of implicit values and priorities that merit careful inspection. The

---

[50] Gillespie, P., (2016). "America's Part-time Work Force Is Huge." CNN Business, April 25, 2016 and found online on July 9, 2021 at America's part-time problem may be permanent (cnn.com).

[51] Glauber, R. K., (2013). "Wanting More but Working Less: Involuntary Part-time Employment and Economic Vulnerability." Carsey Institute, University of New Hampshire. Found online on July 9, 2021 at "Wanting more but working less: involuntary part-time employment and ec" by Rebecca K. Glauber (unh.edu).

[52] Pfeffer, (1998), *op. cit.*

[53] Beer, M., (2009). High Commitment High Performance:

following are eight assumptions that are consistent with the arms-length treatment of employees.

This **arms-length treatment of employees** typically **reflects a corporation's concern for short-term profit taking and cost cutting**, rather than **pursuing the creation of long-term value** for a **firm** and for **customers**.

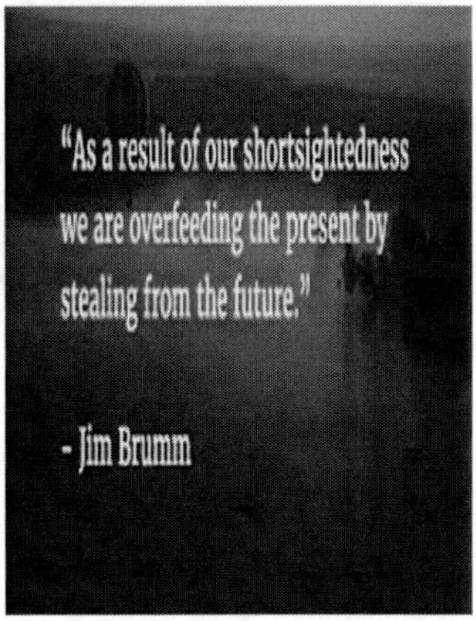

1) Employers Owe no Long-Term Obligation to Their Employees or to Society

This belief views the transactional relationship of employer and employee as purely an economic exchange. Ethically, according to this assumption the relationship of the employer is fully met by compensating the employee for work performed. There is no interpersonal or humanistic obligation of the employer to the employee and the ability of the employee to meet his economic, social, and other needs has no bearing on the employer in society.

Ethically, **according to this assumption the relationship of the employer** is fully **met by monetarily compensating the employee** for work performed. There is **no interpersonal or humanistic obligation** of the employer **to the employee** and **the ability of the employee to meet his economic, social, and other needs** has **no bearing on the employer** in society.

2) An Organization's Short-Term Financial Priorities Justify Minimizing Its Labor Costs

The premise for this assumption is that the economic marketplace has become more competitive and that the primary responsibility of those who lead the organization is to their owners and shareholders. This assumption is based upon the idea that an organization exists to maximize short-term profits for owners, investors, and venture capitalists.

This **assumption** is based upon the idea that **an organization exists to maximize short-term profits** for **owners, investors, and venture capitalists.**

3) Reducing labor costs is best achieved by hiring part-time, temporary, and contract employees

The underlying reality is that insurance, vacation, retirement, sick leave, and holiday costs can all be eliminated by hiring employees who are not full-time and who do not receive such benefits. As a 2018 study by Harvard's Lawrence Katz and Princeton's Alan Krueger reported, 94% of net job growth in the decade between 2005 and 2015 in the United States was due to "alternative work category" employees[54]. As employers have sought to minimize their labor costs, this trend has continued[55].

[54] Katz, L. F. & Krueger, A. B., (2018). "The Rise and Nature of Work Arrangements in the United States, 1995-2015." *Industrial and Labor Relations Review*, Vol. 72, Iss. 2, pp. 382-416.

[55] Investing.com, (2016). "Nearly 95% of All New Jobs During Obama Era Were Part-time, or Contract." Found online on July 9, 2021 at Nearly 95% of all new jobs during Obama era were part-time, or contract By Investing.com.

As a **2018 study** by Harvard's Lawrence Katz and Princeton's Alan Krueger reported, **94% of net job growth in the decade between 2005 and 2015** in the United States was **due to "alternative work category" employees.**

4) Work Tasks Performed by Employees are Easily Accomplished and Require Minimal Skills

For **many positions in the service, retail, and manufacturing industries** believe that the **work performed is relatively low skilled and does not require a great deal of education or training.** Despite this perception, **close to 60 percent of the firms in these groups have reported difficulty** in **finding qualified applicants,** including **one-fourth reporting extreme difficulty.**

For many positions in the service, retail, and manufacturing industries believe that the work performed is relatively low-skilled and does not require a great deal of education or training[56]. Despite this perception, close to 60 percent of the firms in these groups have reported difficulty in finding qualified applicants, including one-fourth reporting extreme difficulty[57]. Low-skilled jobs are defined as jobs requiring only a high school education and one year of actual work experience[58].

5) Employees Can be Easily Replaced and are Essentially Interchangeable

The assumption that employees are interchangeable and universally available has been challenged in the after-math of the COVID-19 virus[59]. Salaries for advertised positions are high but many positions continue to go unfilled[60]. Employers report that even low-skilled positions are not being filled, despite efforts to attract job candidates by increasing wages offered[61] – especially for technically related positions[62].

The assumption that **employees are interchangeable and universally available** has been **challenged in the after-math of the COVID-19 virus. Salaries for advertised positions are high** but **many positions continue to go unfilled.**

[56] Maxwell, Nan L. 2006. "Low-SkilCed Jobs: The Reality Behind the Popular Perceptions." In *The Working Life: The Labor Market for Workers in Low-Skilled Jobs*. Kalamazoo, MI: W.E. Upjohn Institute for Employment Research, pp. 1-23.

[57] *Ibid*.

[58] *Ibid*.

[59] Rhein, N., (2021). "Why Hiring is So Difficult Right Now." *Detroit Today*, June 7, 2021 and found online on July 9, 2021 at Why Hiring Is So Difficult Right Now | WDET.

[60] *Ibid*.

[61] *Ibid*.

[62] *Ibid*.

6) Treating Employees as Participants in an Exchange Relationship Has a Minimal Impact on Individual and Company Morale

Unfortunately, when companies treat employees as commodities or as participants in a purely transactional relationship, the commitment of those employees decreases[63]. Employees are motivated by far more than by compensation[64] and when their employers fail to demonstrate a commitment to their employees' interests, employees tend to feel marginalized and disrespected[65]. Employees treated as valued partners have greater organization commitment and are more productive[66].

Employees are **motivated by far more than by their compensation** and when their **employers fail to demonstrate a commitment to their employees' interests, employees tend to feel marginalized** and disrespected.

7) Establishing a Transactional Relationship with Employees Does Not Negatively Impact Service to Customers

There is a well-established principle of employee relationships that Stephen R. Covey has articulated about customer service. Dr. Covey explained that employees will not treat their customers any better than they are treated by their organization[67]. Treating employees with indifferent interest in their personal and professional needs is likely to result in those same employees treating customers with that same indifference[68].

---

[63] Pfeffer, (1998), *op. cit.*

[64] Collins, J. & Porras, J. I., (2004). *Built to Last: Successful Habits of Visionary Companies.* New York: HarperCollins.

[65] Hughes, C., (2012). *Valuing People and Technology in the Workplace: A Competitive Advantage Framework.* Hershey, PA: IGI Global.

[66] Block, P., (2013). *Stewardship: Choosing Service Over Self-Interest.* San Francisco, CA: Jossey-Bass.

[67] Covey, S. R., (1992). *Principle-Centered Leadership.* New York: Touchstone Printing.

[68] Simpson, S. & Cacioppe, R. (2001), "Unwritten Ground Rules: Transforming Organization Culture to Achieve Key Business Objectives and Outstanding Customer Service." *Leadership & Organization Development Journal*, Vol. 22 No. 8, pp. 394-401.

Treating employees with **indifferent interest in their personal and professional needs** is likely to **result in those same employees treating customers with that same indifference.**

8) Treating Employees as Arm's-Length Employees Does Not Affect Employee Creativity and Innovation

Assuming that treating employees as commodities will not affect their commitment and their willingness to be creative and innovative is a dangerous and erroneous assumption[69]. Because the ability to be innovative is so important to achieving a competitive advantage in the modern economy, it is in companies' best interests to promote creativity and innovation in order to take advantage of employees' individual abilities[70].

Because **the ability to be innovative is so important** to achieving a **competitive advantage in the modern economy,** it is **in companies' best interests to promote creativity and innovation** in order to take **advantage of employees' individual abilities.**

[69] Covey, S. R., (1992), *op. cit.*

[70] Christensen, C. M., (2016). *The Innovator's Dilemma: When New Technologies Cause Great Firms to Fail*. Boston, MA: Harvard Business Review Press.

These eight assumptions about the rationale for treating employees in a simply transactional arms-length relationship are inconsistent with a company's best interests. As noted by a number of scholars, the culture and values of an organization greatly influence are typically mirrored by those who work for those organizations[71]. Consequently, leaders, managers, and supervisors who treat employees as commodities have seen their employees respond with low commitment, loyalty, and trust[72].

These eight **assumptions about how leaders interact with employees are inconsistent** with **creating high trust and high-performance organizations** and are **in conflict** with the pursuit of a **creating a competitive advantage**.

Leading with Passion

In contrast with an arms-length approach to relating with employees, highly successful leaders are committed to employees and understand the importance of demonstrating that commitment. Leading with passion requires five factors that can enable leaders to establish relationships that inspire employees and empower them to make a contribution that adds value to an organization. Each of the five factors is briefly explained.

---

[71] See, for example, Schein, E. H. & Schein, P. A., (2016). Organizational Culture and Leadership (6th ed.). San Francisco, CA: Jossey-Bass and Simpson & Cacioppe, (2001), *op. cit.*

[72] Clifton & Harter, (2019), *op. cit.*

- ***Setting a Personal Example***

Leading others and establishing a personal relationship begins with a leader's willingness to model the values, principles, and standards that (s)he advocates to others[73]. Personal example includes treating others as valued partners in the process of improving an organization[74] and demonstrating an interest in others' welfare, growth, and wholeness[75] - an obligation described as a covenantal duty of leaders by many leadership experts[76].

Personal example includes **treating others as valued owners and partners** in the process of **improving an organization** and **demonstrating an interest in others' welfare, growth, and wholeness** -- an obligation described as **a covenantal duty of leaders** by many leadership experts.

- ***Recognizing Others' Contributions***

Leaders who recognize the importance of others in organizations go out of their way to give credit to those who help an organization to succeed[77]. The primary reason why employees leave organizations is because their leaders fail to recognize their efforts, according to research by Mental Health America[78]. Extensive worldwide research conducted by the Gallup research

---

[73] Kouzes, J. M. & Posner, B. Z., (2017). *The Leadership Challenge: How to Make Extraordinary Things Happen in Organizations* (7th ed.). San Francisco, CA: Jossey-Bass.

[74] Block, (2013), *op. cit.*

[75] Pfeffer, (1998), *op. cit.*

[76] See, for example, DePree, M., (2004). *Leadership is an Art*. New York: Crown Publishers and Covey, S. R., (2004). *The 8th Habit: From Effectiveness to Greatness*. New York: Free Press.

[77] Collins, J., (2001). *Good to Great: Why Some Companies Make the Leap. . . And Others Don't*. New York: HarperCollins.

[78] Schwantes, M., (2018). "A New Study Reveals 70 Percent of Employees Say They Are Actively Looking for a New Job. Here's the Reason in Five Words." *Inc.*, Dec. 4, 2018 and

group has confirmed that when employees are not recognized and supported by their leaders, managers, and supervisors, their commitment to their organization decreases along with their performance[79].

Extensive worldwide research conducted by the Gallup research group has confirmed that **when employees are not recognized and supported** by their leaders, managers, and supervisors, **their commitment to their organization decreases along with their performance.**

- ***Holding Supervisors Accountable***

Supervisors and managers frequently lack the skills to establish healthy relationships with employees – and the selection and training of those who supervise others is often top management's fault[80]. According to Gallup research, the low morale and poor performance of employees is unequivocally due to organizational leaders failing to create healthy relationships with employees when they do not properly hire qualified managers and supervisors and train them to treat employees with dignity and respect[81].

---

found online on July 10, 2021 at A New Study Reveals 70 Percent of Workers Say They Are Actively Looking for a New Job. Here's the Reason in 5 Words | Inc.com.

[79] Clifton & Harter, (2019), *op. cit.*

[80] Schwantes, M. (2017). "Research: Why 70 Percent of Employees Aren't Working to Their Full Potential Comes Down to 1 Simple Reason." Inc., November 22, 2017 and found online on July 10, 2021 at Research: Why 70 Percent of Employees Aren't Working to Their Full Potential Comes Down to 1 Simple Reason | Inc.com.

[81] Clifton & Harter, (2019), *op. cit.*

The **low morale and poor performance** of employees **is unequivocally due to organizational leaders failing to create healthy relationships** with employees **when they do not hire qualified managers and supervisors** and train **them to treat employees with dignity and respect.**

- ***Valuing Each Individual***

When leaders, managers, and supervisors understand the needs of each employee and treat them with a commitment to their best interests, they demonstrate that they value those individuals[82]. Moreover, employees pay close attention to the consistency and fairness of leaders and note that how one person is treated reflects how all individuals are valued by their organization[83].

Employees pay close attention to the **consistency and fairness of leaders** and note that **how one person is treated reflects how all individuals are valued** by their organization.

[82] Caldwell, C. & Anderson, V., (2019). "Love: The Heart of Leadership, Introduction and Overview." In C. Caldwell & V. Anderson, (Eds.), *Leading with Love*. Hauppauge, NY: NOVA Publishing.

[83] Covey, (1992), *op. cit.*

- ***Fostering Continuous Improvement***

Helping employees to improve their skills, their performance, and their promotability benefits the organization as well as each individual[84]. Investing in employees and their success, helping them to "find their voice," and empowering them to achieve their highest potential is viewed by many leadership scholars as a moral obligation of leaders and organizations[85].

Investing in employees and their success, **helping them to "find their voice,"** and **empowering them to achieve their highest potential** is viewed by many leadership scholars as a **moral responsibility of leaders and organizations**.

Each of these five factors helps leaders and organizations to create an organizational culture that communicates to employees that they are valued and that their performance contributes in material ways to their organizations' successes. The message to employees is that their leaders care about them and recognize their significance as individuals, rather than simply as contributors to their companies' bottom line profits. Leaders who care deeply about their employees' growth and development demonstrate the passion that wins the commitment, loyalty, and trust that matches their own personal commitment.

---

[84] Johnson, D., Citera, M. & Wrench, J. S., (2014). *Training and Development: The Intersection of Communication and Talent Development in the Modern Workplace*. Dubuque, IA: Kendall Hunt Publishing.

[85] Covey, (2004), *op. cit.* and DePree, (2004), *op. cit.*

Leaders who care deeply about their employees' growth and development demonstrate the passion that wins the loyalty and trust that matches their own personal commitment.

Ten Recommendations

Establishing relationships that communicate the value of people sends a powerful message. That message is that the people with whom leaders work are not arm's-length associates paid to simply accomplish tasks but are fully involved owners and partners in their organizations' successes[86]. We suggest that those who care about employees as "Yous" rather than as "Its" can affirm that message by adopting the ten recommendations included here.

1) Focus on and Identify Others' Personal Goals

When people are understood and assisted to achieve their goals, they recognize that their priorities are acknowledged and respected[87]. Validating the importance of others' goals communicates to them that they are personally appreciated. When a leader or supervisor can help an employee to achieve her/his personal and professional goals, a bond is created that strengthens the employee's commitment to the organization[88].

---

[86] Block, P. (2013). *Stewardship: Choosing Service Over Self-Interest*. San Francisco, CA: Jossey-Bass.

[87] LeBlanc, L., Sellers, T. & Ala'I, S., (2020). *Building and Sustaining Meaningful and Effective Relationships as a Supervisor and Mentor*. Hudson, NY: Sloan Educational Publishing.

[88] *Ibid*.

2) Meet Weekly with Each Direct Report to Coach And Support

Gallup's Chairman, Jim Clifton, discovered that the most effective leaders coach others on a weekly basis in establishing relationships that inspire, support, and motivate others[89]. Making the effort to connect and be supportive about others' goals on an individual basis each week sends a clear message that the person being coached is truly viewed as an important contributor to the organization[90]. More importantly, a supportive coaching approach is far superior than a traditional performance appraisal meeting that typically focuses on areas where improvement is needed[91].

[89] Clifton, J., (2021). "Gallup Finds a Silver Bullet: Coach Me Once Per Week." Gallup, May 27, 2021 and found online on July 11, 2021 at Gallup Finds a Silver Bullet: Coach Me Once Per Week.

[90] *Ibid.*

[91] Ellinger, A. D., Ellinger, A. E., Hamlin, R. G., & Beattie, R. S. (2010). "Achieving Improved Performance through Managerial Coaching." In R. Watkins & D. Leigh (Eds.), *Handbook for the Selection and Implementation of Human Performance Interventions*. San Francisco, CA: Jossey-Bass, pp. 275-298.

3) Ask About and Listen to Each Person's Concerns

Caring genuinely about an employee's concerns is communicated by asking for feedback, listening to understand the context and rationale, and following up with actions that effectively address that employee's perspective[92]. Effective listening requires clearly identifying the message conveyed by each employee and responding in a manner that demonstrates that the meaning behind that message is understood and acknowledged[93].

Caring genuinely about an employee's concerns is communicated by asking for feedback and listening

4) Model the Commitment to Personal Self-Improvement

Modeling personal improvement by a leader's example enables that leader to be more successful in encouraging others to also improve[94]. Self-improvement efforts can come in many forms. One of the most effective ways for a leader to model her/his commitment to improving is by actively participating in employee training programs and applying the principles learned in partnership with other employees.

[92] Becker, E. F. & Wortmann, J., (2009). *Mastering Communication at Work: How to Lead, Manage, and Influence*. Boston, MA: McGraw-Hill Education.

[93] *Ibid.*

[94] Kouzes & Posner, (2017), *op. cit.*

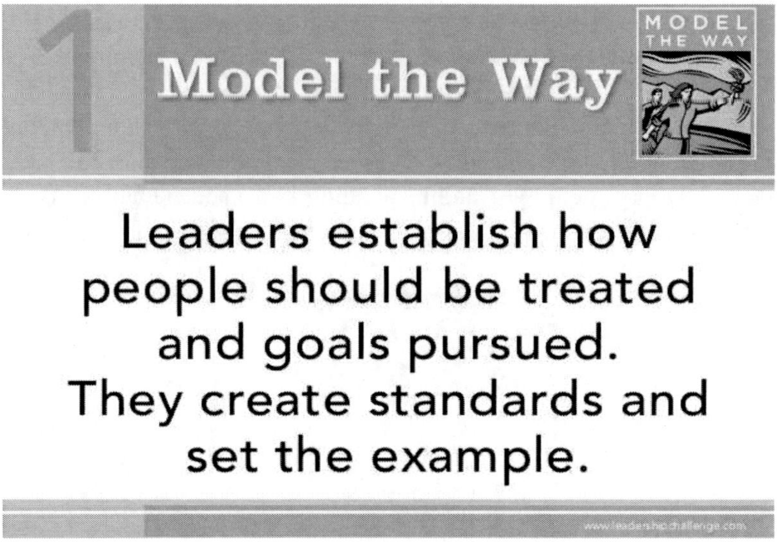

5) Create Opportunities to Support Others' Growth

By implementing policies and programs that support others' growth, a leader demonstrates that (s)he is committed to others' improvement. As leaders and organizations invest in employees' personal improvement with resources and personal effort, they reinforce the importance of continuous improvement and constant learning[95] – and they also affirm to employees that they are valued by their organization.

[95] Senge, P. M., (2006). *The Fifth Discipline: The Art & Practice of the Learning Organization*. New York: Doubleday.

6) Assist Others to Understand How They Add Value

Establishing metrics for assessing value-added and helping others to understand how they contribute to an organization's success is a vital skill that empowers employees and assists them to focus their efforts[96]. Helping employees to then increase their effectiveness in contribution to their organization's success enables leaders to assist those employees to make an increased contribution.

7) Focus on Positive Achievements Rather Than Mistakes

Emphasizing employee strengths and helping them to continue to improve in areas where they have unique abilities enables an organization to excel while also creating a stronger bond with those highly-skilled individuals[97]. Rather than identifying employee shortcomings, emphasizing strengths builds confidence, increases productivity, strengthens relationships with supervisors, and improves employee commitment[98].

---

[96] FITZ-ENZ, J., (2009). *The ROI of Human Capital: Measuring the Economic Value of Employee Performance*. New York: AMACOM.

[97] Lee, C., (2020). *Performance Conversations: How to Use Questions to Coach Employees, Improve Productivity, and Boost Confidence (Without Appraisals)*. Alexandria, VA: Society for Human Resource Management.

[98] *Ibid*.

Rather than identifying employee **shortcomings, emphasizing strengths** builds **confidence, increases productivity, strengthens relationships with supervisors**, and **improves employee commitment**.

8) Reward Successes on a Timely Basis

Acknowledging and rewarding accomplishments and important achievements on a timely basis reinforce those successes and demonstrate the appreciation of the organization[99]. Delaying recognition of outstanding achievements can actually send a message that what has been accomplished is not fully appreciated[100]. Timely recognition of accomplishments also communicates to others that their efforts are valued[101].

Timely recognition **of accomplishments** communicates **to others that their** efforts are valued

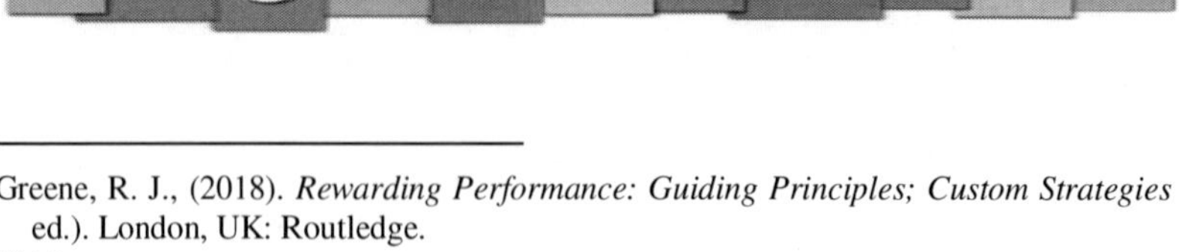

[99] Greene, R. J., (2018). *Rewarding Performance: Guiding Principles; Custom Strategies* (2nd ed.). London, UK: Routledge.
[100] *Ibid.*
[101] *Ibid.*

9) Create Programs and Policies that Cement the Culture

As leaders seek to build relationships with others, their intentions are most effective when matched with programs and policies that align with espoused values[102]. Establishing credibility and sustaining improved relationships are strengthened when leaders and supervisors match their beliefs about the importance of relationships with policies, programs, and systems that empower, engage, and enable employees.[103]

As leaders seek to build relationships with others, their intentions are most effective when matched with programs and policies that align with espoused values.

10) Pursue Constant Improvement

The most effective leaders who constantly improve their organizations recognize the importance of involving employees at all levels and engaging them in the continuous improvement process[104]. These leaders also hold themselves accountable for creating personal relationships that communicate to employees that they each matter to their organization's success.

---

[102] Schein & Schein, (2016), *op. cit.*

[103] Anderson, V. & Caldwell, C., (2019). "Transforming People: Creating a Culture of Change." In C. Caldwell & V. Anderson, *Human Resource Management: A Transformative Approach.* Hauppauge, NY: NOVA Publishing, Chapter 7.

[104] Pfeffer, (1998), *op. cit.*

The most effective leaders who constantly improve their organizations recognize the importance of involving employees at all levels and engaging them in the continuous improvement process

The degree to which leaders, managers, and supervisors incorporate these recommendations, together with the five factors for leading with passion, can exponentially increase the level of trust that they develop with employees and increase employee willingness to reciprocate that trust with extra-mile effort.

Conclusion

Despite the beliefs of many of today's managers, supervisors, and leaders, the evidence confirms that treating employees as commodities hired to complete assigned tasks fails to unlock employee potential. Ironically, the evidence confirming the importance of treating employees as people, as opposed to "human resources" or "human capital," has been available for decades.[105] Unfortunately, it is also true that organizations are apparently poorly led and do not understand the negative results that come from treating employees as commodities.[106]

Until those who lead, manage, and supervise employees move beyond transactional assumptions about employee relations, organizations will continue to struggle. Leading with passion requires that leaders adopt a transformational or transformative approach to employees that seeks to help employees to grow, treats them as valued partners, and honors the leader's obligation to help employees become the best version of themselves. The good

[105] *Ibid.*
[106] Clifton & Harter, (2019), *op. cit.*

news is that the evidence suggests that this more humane approach to human relationships pays off in better quality, lower turnover, better customer service, and higher profits.

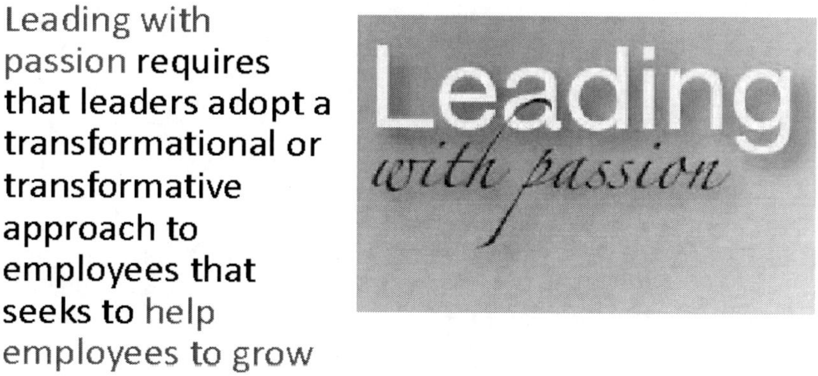

Until those who lead, manage, and supervise employees move beyond transactional assumptions about employee relations, organizations will continue to struggle. Leading with passion requires that leaders adopt a transformational or transformative approach to employees that seeks to help employees to grow, treats them as valued partners, and honors the leader's obligation to help employees become the best version of themselves. The good news is that the evidence suggests that this more humane approach to human relationships pays off in better quality, lower turnover, better customer service, and higher profits.

References

Anderson, V. & Caldwell, C., (2019). "Transforming People: Creating a Culture of Change." In C. Caldwell & V. Anderson, *Human Resource Management: A Transformative Approach*. Hauppauge, NY: NOVA Publishing, Chapter 7.

Becker, E. F. & Wortmann, J., (2009). *Mastering Communication at Work: How to Lead, Manage, and Influence*. Boston, MA: McGraw-Hill Education.

Block, P., (2013). *Stewardship: Choosing Service Over Self-Interest*. San Francisco, CA: Jossey-Bass.

Burns, J. M., (2010). *Leadership*. New York: Harper Perennial.

Caldwell, C. & Anderson, V., (2019). "Love: The Heart of Leadership, Introduction and Overview." In C. Caldwell & V. Anderson, (Eds.), *Leading with Love*. Hauppauge, NY: NOVA Publishing.

Caldwell, C., Floyd, L. A., Taylor, J. & Woodard, B. (2014). "Beneficence as a Source of Competitive Advantage." *Journal of Management Development*, Vol. 33, Iss. 10, pp. 1057-1069.

Christensen, C. M., (2016). *The Innovator's Dilemma: When New Technologies Cause Great Firms to Fail*. Boston, MA: Harvard Business Review Press.

Clifton, J., (2021). "Gallup Finds a Silver Bullet: Coach Me Once Per Week." Gallup, May 27, 2021 and found online on July 11, 2021 at Gallup Finds a Silver Bullet: Coach Me Once Per Week.

Clifton, J. & Harter, J., (2019). *It's the Manager*. Omaha, NE: Gallup Press.

Collins, J. & Porras, J. I., (2004). *Built to Last: Successful Habits of Visionary Companies*. New York: HarperCollins.

Collins, J., (2001). *Good to Great: Why Some Companies Make the Leap. . . And Others Don't*. New York: HarperCollins.

Covey, S. R., (1992). *Principle-Centered Leadership*. New York: Touchstone Printing.

DePree, M., (2004). *Leadership is an Art*. New York: Crown Publishers and Covey, S. R., (2004). *The 8th Habit: From Effectiveness to Greatness*. New York: Free Press.

Edelman, (2021). "Edelman Trust Barometer 2021." Found online on July 4, 2021 at 2021 Edelman Trust Barometer | Edelman.

Ellinger, A. D., Ellinger, A. E., Hamlin, R. G., & Beattie, R. S. (2010). "Achieving Improved Performance through Managerial Coaching." In R. Watkins & D. Leigh (Eds.), *Handbook for the Selection and Implementation of Human Performance*

Fitz-Enz, J., (2009). *The ROI of Human Capital: Measuring the Economic Value of Employee Performance*. New York: AMACOM.

Gillespie, P., (2016). "America's Part-time Work Force Is Huge." CNN Business, April 25, 2016 and found online on July 9, 2021 at America's part-time problem may be permanent (cnn.com).

Glauber, R. K., (2013). "Wanting More but Working Less: Involuntary Part-time Employment and Economic Vulnerability." Carsey Institute, University of New Hampshire. Found online on July 9, 2021 at "Wanting more but working less: involuntary part-time employment and ec" by Rebecca K. Glauber (unh.edu).

Greene, R. J., (2018). *Rewarding Performance: Guiding Principles; Custom Strategies* (2nd ed.). London, UK: Routledge.

Hellebuyck, M., Nguyen, T. Halphern, M., Fritze, D. & Kennedy, J., (2017). *Mind the Workplace*. Lancaster, CA: Mental Health America.

Hughes, C., (2012). *Valuing People and Technology in the Workplace: A Competitive Advantage Framework*. Hershey, PA: IGI Global.

Investing.com, (2016). "Nearly 95% of All New Jobs During Obama Era Were Part-time, or Contract." Found online on July 9, 2021 at Nearly 95% of all new jobs during Obama era were part-time, or contract By Investing.com.

Johnson, D., Citera, M. & Wrench, J. S., (2014). *Training and Development: The Intersection of Communication and Talent Development in the Modern Workplace*. Dubuque, IA: Kendall Hunt Publishing.

Katz, L. F. & Krueger, A. B., (2018). "The Rise and Nature of Work Arrangements in the United States, 1995-2015." *Industrial and Labor Relations Review*, Vol. 72, Iss. 2, pp. 382-416.

Kouzes, J. M. & Posner, B. Z., (2017). *The Leadership Challenge: How to Make Extraordinary Things Happen in Organizations* (7th ed.). San Francisco, CA: Jossey-Bass.

LeBlanc, L., Sellers, T. & Ala'I, S., (2020). *Building and Sustaining Meaningful and Effective Relationships as a Supervisor and Mentor*. Hudson, NY: Sloan Educational Publishing.

Lee, C., (2020). *Performance Conversations: How to Use Questions to Coach Employees, Improve Productivity, and Boost Confidence (Without Appraisals)*. Alexandria, VA: Society for Human Resource Management.

Maudlin, J., (2021). "4 Economic Challenges for 2021." *Forbes*, January 18, 2021 and found online on July 4, 2021 at 4 Economic Challenges For 2021 (forbes.com).

Maxwell, Nan L. 2006. "Low-SkilCed Jobs: The Reality Behind the Popular Perceptions." In *The Working Life: The Labor Market for Workers in Low-Skilled Jobs*. Kalamazoo, MI: W.E. Upjohn Institute for Employment Research, pp. 1-23.

Murray, J., (2020). "What is an Arms Length Transaction?" *the balance small business*, October 30, 2020 and found online on July 5, 2021 at An Arm's Length Transaction: What Is It? (thebalancesmb.com),

Pfeffer, J., (1998). *The Human Equation: Building Profits by Putting People First*. Boston, MA: Harvard Business Review Press.

Rhein, N., (2021). "Why Hiring is So Difficult Right Now." *Detroit Today*, June 7, 2021 and found online on July 9, 2021 at Why Hiring Is So Difficult Right Now | WDET.

Schein, E. H. & Schein, P. A., (2016). *Organizational Culture and Leadership* (6th ed.). San Francisco, CA: Jossey-Bass and Simpson & Cacioppe, (2001),

Schwantes, M., (2018). "A New Study Reveals 70 Percent of Employees Say They Are Actively Looking for a New Job. Here's the Reason in Five Words." *Inc.*, Dec. 4, 2018 and found online on July 10, 2021 at A New Study Reveals 70 Percent of Workers Say They Are Actively Looking for a New Job. Here's the Reason in 5 Words | Inc.com.

Schwantes, M. (2017). "Research: Why 70 Percent of Employees Aren't Working to Their Full Potential Comes Down to 1 Simple Reason." Inc., November 22, 2017 and found online on July 10, 2021 at Research: Why 70 Percent of Employees Aren't Working to Their Full Potential Comes Down to 1 Simple Reason | Inc.com.

Senge, P. M., (2006). *The Fifth Discipline: The Art & Practice of the Learning Organization*. New York: Doubleday.

Simpson, S. & Cacioppe, R. (2001), "Unwritten Ground Rules: Transforming Organization Culture to Achieve Key Business Objectives and Outstanding Customer Service." *Leadership & Organization Development Journal*, Vol. 22 No. 8, pp. 394-401.

Sturt & Nordstrom, (2018). "10 Shocking Workplace Stats You Need to Know." Forbes, March 8, 2018 and found online on September 30, 2020 at https://www.forbes.com/sites/davidsturt/2018/03/08/10-shocking-workplace-stats-you-need-to-know/#2a90c892f3af.

Chapter 3

Leading with Commitment

As a leadership quality, commitment demonstrates the ability to stay focused and to keep working – despite obstacles, disappointments, personal circumstances, or changing conditions[107]. Commitment incorporates the ability to persist and persevere by being fully invested in achieving a desired outcome[108]. As leaders fulfill a commitment, they communicate to those with whom they are interacting that the outcome they seek truly matters. Unfortunately, although commitments are often made in relationships, they are not always honored.

As a leadership quality, commitment demonstrates the ability to **stay focused** and to **keep working – despite obstacles, disappointments, personal circumstances,** or **changing conditions.**

The purpose of this chapter is to examine the nature of commitment and the factors upon which it is based. We begin the chapter by defining the nature of commitment and identifying its importance as a characteristic of effective leaders. We identify ten reasons why commitments are not always honored

[107] Dethmer, J., Chapman, D. & Klemp, K. W., (2015). *The 15 Commitments of Conscious Leadership: A New Paradigm for Sustainable Success*. Muncie, IN: The Conscious Leadership Group.

[108] *Ibid.*

and explain why keeping commitments is often difficult. We then identify six antecedents to commitment and describe how those antecedents influence the willingness and ability to sustain individual effort in the pursuit of an intended goal. We include in that assessment the role of commitment in reflecting the individual identity of an individual and the strength of the values that determine action. We close the chapter with encouragement to leaders to understand that to which they are committed and to appreciate the impact of their choices on their ability to lead effectively.

Understanding Commitment

A commitment is 1) the willingness to invest the time, resources, and energy required to accomplish an intended outcome or 2) the promise that is made to oneself or to another individual to honor a specific responsibility. A commitment is made up of an intended action that has value when it is converted into a sustained action[109].

A **commitment** is 1) the **willingness to invest the time, resources, and energy** required to **accomplish an intended outcome** or 2) the **promise** that is **made to oneself or to another individual** to **honor** a **specific responsibility**.

Lacking the intended behavior, a commitment undermines trust and negates a relationship – leaving the party to whom the commitment was made to feel disappointed, cautious, and unwilling to trust the party making the commitment. Breaching a commitment is a betrayal of trust, in addition to having other potential legal and relationship-based consequences. Although

[109] *Ibid.*

commitments may have serious consequences, they are often not honored for a multitude of reasons[110].

Although commitments may have serious consequences, they are often not honored for a multitude of reasons.

Commitment has its roots in the Latin and comes from *com*, meaning "with" and *mittere*, meaning "to send." In common usage, there are nine different definitions of the word commitment and its meaning depends entirely on the context in which the word is used. Commitment can mean any of the following[111].

1. The doing or perpetration of a blunder or crime. A commission of an action.
2. A warrant or order for the imprisonment of someone. In legal terms, a mittimus.
3. The act of committing or putting in charge, keeping, or trust; consignment, especially committing to prison.
4. The act of pledging or engaging; the act of exposing, endangering, or compromising; also, the state of being pledged or engaged.
5. The act of referring or entrusting to a committee for consideration and report; as, the commitment of a petition or bill.
6. The act of binding oneself, either intellectually or emotionally, to a course of action.

---

[110] *Ibid.*

[111] See "Commitment." *Fine Dictionary*. Found online on October 20, 2021 at commitment - definition, etymology and usage, examples and related words (finedictionary.com).

7. The engagement by contract involving a financial or personal obligation.
8. The trait of sincere and steadfast fixity of purpose.
9. A message that communicates a pledge or promise.

The focus of this chapter is on the last four of these definitions and the importance of those definitions of commitment in interpersonal relationships and in organizations.

As **applied to the relationship between a leader and members** of an organization, **commitment involves a leader's dedication** to a **specific course of action** and her/his **willingness to be accountable** for the **responsibilities associated**.

As applied to the relationship between a leader and members of an organization, commitment involves a leader's dedication to a specific course of action and her/his willingness to be accountable for the responsibilities associated[112]. Based upon his research associated with commitment and effective leadership, Jim Collins made the following observation.

> "The kind of commitment I find among the best performers across virtually every field is a single-minded passion for what they do, an unwavering desire for excellence in the way they think and the way they work."

---

[112] Catano, V.M., Pond, M. and Kelloway, E. K., (2001), "Exploring Commitment and Leadership in Volunteer Organizations," *Leadership & Organization Development Journal*, Vol. 22 No. 6, pp. 256-263.

It is this pursuit of excellence and the unyielding desire to accomplish a worthy goal that enables leaders to focus their efforts and demonstrate the "fixity of purpose" that represents that specific element of commitment.

> **Like other** individual traits, **commitment may best be understood as a continuum** reflecting the **degree of that person's willingness to follow through and fulfill an expected obligation.**

In relationships, the level of commitment may sometimes vary with regard to the extent that an individual will personally invest her/his efforts to achieve a goal or to honor a promise that (s)he may make. Like other individual traits, commitment may best be understood as a continuum reflecting the degree of that person's willingness to follow through and fulfill an expected obligation. Figure 1 identifies five examples of differing levels of personal investment in a commitment continuum.

Lip Service	Conditional Agreement	Contractual Promise	Earnest Willingness	Unqualified Dedication
No real intention to comply	Intend to comply under favorable conditions	Compliance is intended but willing to pay a penalty for a breach	Seeks to give a genuine effort to perform within realistic conditions	Willing to go the extra mile and to do all possible to honor obligation

Figure 1. Commitment Continuum.

The degree of an individual's commitment may vary and will equate with that person's fidelity in honoring a duty, commitment, promise, or obligation. The level of commitment demonstrated will generally correspond with the regard in which that person is held by others to whom a commitment is owed[113].

The level of commitment demonstrated will generally correspond with the regard in which that person is held by others to whom a commitment is owed.

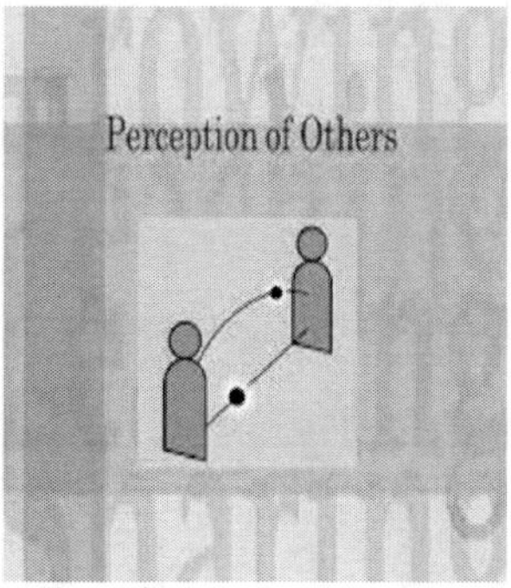

Why Commitments Aren't Kept

As suggested by Figure 1, commitments may sometimes be made but may not necessarily be kept. Although honoring a commitment is often vitally important and the failure to fulfill an obligation may have serious consequences, the failure to keep a commitment – whether to oneself, to another person, or to God – can occur for any number of reasons.

Although **honoring a commitment** is often **vitally important** and the **failure to fulfill an obligation** may have **serious consequences**, the **failure to keep a commitment** – whether to oneself, to another person, or to God – can **occur for any number of reasons.**

[113] *Ibid.*

The following are ten of the most common reasons why commitments are not kept.

1. *A lack of ability* – A person may make a commitment and intend to fulfill it but lack the ability to complete what is promised.
2. *A lack of self-confidence* – Accomplishing a task may involve obstacles that an individual may believe exceed her/his capabilities.
3. *Inadequate preparation* – Completing a task or achieving a desired result may require resources and/or a plan of action for which an individual has not properly prepared.
4. *Inadequate desire* – A person may be capable of performing a task that (s)he had committed to completing but lacks the desire to perform the task.
5. *Insufficient expectations* – The completion of a task or the fulfilling of a promise may not be perceived as resulting in an outcome that is worth the resources and effort required.
6. *A desire to look good* – A promise or commitment may have been made out of a desire to impress others and to look good in their eyes, without a real intent to complete an obligation.
7. *Inability to focus* – Circumstances may arise that impede an individual's ability to focus the effort required to perform a task effectively.
8. *Personal selfishness* – A person may either change her/his mind or decide to not honor a promise out of personal self-interest.
9. *Basic dishonesty* – Being dishonest with oneself or with others is increasingly common as a cause of the failure to keep a commitment.
10. *Insufficient integrity* – The failure to honor a commitment made sometimes is simply related to a deficiency in moral identity or personal integrity to do what one promises.

Whatever the reason for failing to keep a commitment may be, the result is inevitably the breakdown in trust – whether that occurs in a relationship, within an organization, or simply a commitment made to oneself or to God. That diminishment of trust typically will have an impact on the party to whom the commitment was made – but it also can directly affect the person who fails to keep her/his word.

Whatever the reason for failing to keep a commitment may be, the result is inevitably the breakdown in trust— whether that occurs in a relationship, within an organization, or simply a commitment made to oneself or to God.

The person who fails to keep a commitment will sometimes justify that failure by making the claim that external circumstances have occurred that made honoring a promised performance impossible or unduly difficult. That rationalization is typically an attempt to excuse a failure to honor an obligation and duties owed as part of an existing relationship[114]. Understanding the specific reason why a commitment has not been honored can help individuals to identify patterns in their choices and decisions that hurt their relationships with others[115].

Understanding the specific reason why a commitment has not been honored can help individuals to identify patterns in their choices and decisions that hurt their relationships with others.

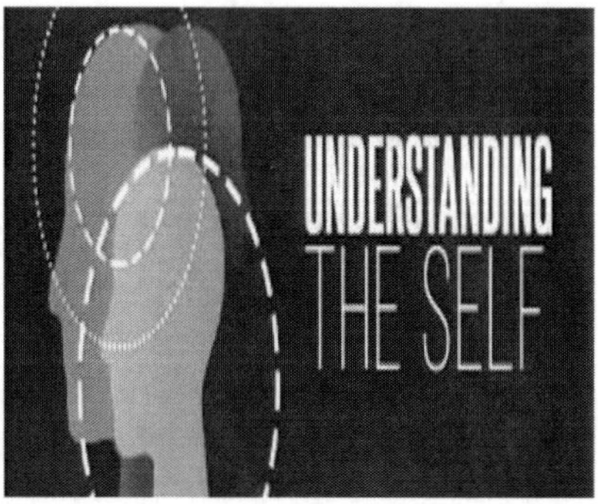

[114] The Arbinger Institute, (2020). *The Anatomy of Peace: Resolving the Heart of Conflict* (3rd ed.). Oakland, CA: Berrett-Koehler Publishers.

[115] *Ibid.*

Antecedents to Commitment

Commitments can be made to others for a multitude of reasons and are common to each person. Whether a commitment involves an obligation made to a friend, the promises associated with the covenant of marriage, a legal contract to purchase something of value, or a well-meaning intention to contact someone at a certain time, the associated elements of that commitment are present – although typically not consciously understood or acknowledged.

Whether a commitment involves an **obligation** made to a friend, the promises associated with the **covenant of marriage**, a **legal contract** to purchase something of value, or a **well-meaning intention** to contact someone at a certain time, the **associated elements** of that commitment are **going to be present** – although **typically not consciously understood or acknowledged**

The following are six antecedents that are typically in play whenever a commitment is made between two parties[116].

A Perceived Obligation

The nature of a commitment is that it contains an underlying ethical responsibility with an obligation owed to the party to whom the commitment is made. This obligation is often subtly acknowledged between the parties and is often associated with their past experiences and their interpersonal or professional relationship. The nature of the obligation may not always be consciously expressed, but it typically plays an important role in any commitment.

---

[116] Dethmer, J., Chapman, D. & Klemp, K. W., (2015), *op. cit.*

The nature of a commitment is that it contains an underlying ethical responsibility with an obligation owed to the party to whom the commitment is made.

A Benefit Expected

Inevitably, whenever a commitment is made the parties involved have a quid pro quo relationship in which the person who makes a promise expects that (s)he will obtain a benefit in return[117]. That benefit may or may not have already been enjoyed or it may simply be made out of a desire to maintain or improve the relationship that exists. Again, this benefit may not necessarily be specifically expressed between the parties – but it nonetheless exists.

Inevitably, whenever a commitment is made the parties involved have a quid pro quo relationship in which the person who makes a promise expects that (s)he will obtain a benefit in return.

[117] Vroom, V. H., (1994). *Work and Motivation*. San Francisco, CA: Jossey-Bass.

The Desire to Respond

The party who is willing to make a commitment does so because (s)he acknowledges in a formal or informal way that (s)he wishes to fulfill an obligation or create a benefit for the other party. The motivation for the commitment may have any of several underlying intentions, but the party who makes the commitment affirmatively communicates her/his desire to honor a perceived responsibility. That desire may also be motivated by a direct request from the other party.

The party who is willing to make a commitment does so because (s)he acknowledges in a formal or informal way that (s)he wishes to fulfill an obligation or create a benefit for the other party.

Perceptions about Self

Implicit in the intention to undertake a perceived responsibility is an individual's perception of herself or himself – especially her/his capacity to honor a commitment and perform as expected. That commitment about personal capacity includes a subjective evaluation of the challenges to be faced, the benefits to accrue, and the costs required to complete the commitment.

Implicit in the intention to undertake a perceived responsibility is **an individual's perception of herself or himself**– especially her/his **capacity to honor a commitment** and **perform as expected.**

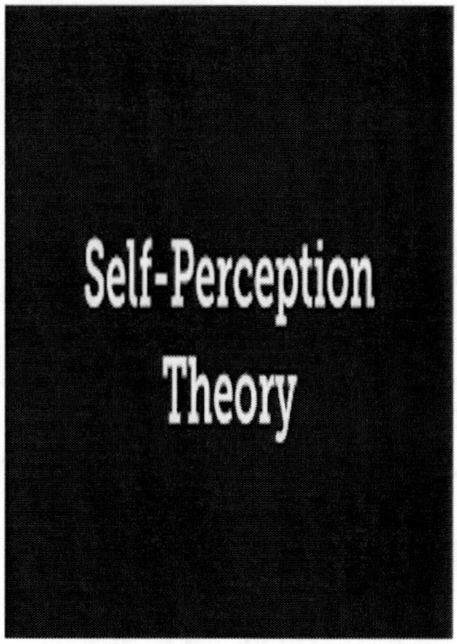

The Willingness to Perform

Each person making a commitment undertakes to perform for the benefit of another party based upon some degree of obligation. The commitment made reflects the desire to honor a responsibility owed to another party that the committing individual agrees to undertake. Sometimes the willingness to perform an action is reluctant, or even intended to simply appease the other party, rather than reflecting a genuine commitment to complete the expected performance.

Each person making a commitment **undertakes to perform for the benefit** of another party **based upon some degree of obligation.**

The Intention to Act

The intention to perform a specific act is conveyed by the party making the commitment – even if that commitment is made begrudgingly. The expressed intention to act may be conveyed as a conditional promise or as part of a contractual duty. This intention to perform may be expressed verbally, in writing, or even non-verbally and may be conveyed despite the fact that the party making the commitment has no intention to actually perform.

The expressed intention to act may be conveyed as a conditional promise or as part of a contractual duty.

As individuals consciously reflect on these six antecedents to making a commitment, they increase their awareness of how they respond in relationships and can thoughtfully address the factors that influence the commitments that they make. Understanding the nature of commitments at the conscious level increases self-awareness and can decrease self-deception behaviors that often undermine relationships[118].

Identity and Commitment

Self-awareness about commitment can also be enhanced by understanding the nature of the identity and its impact on intentions and behaviors. Figure 2, provided following, is an explanation associated with the identity that clarifies

---

[118] Caldwell, C. (2009). "Identity, Self-Deception, and Self-Awareness: Ethical Implications for Leaders and Organizations." *Journal of Business Ethics*, Vol. 90, Supp. 3, pp. 393-406.

the relationship between beliefs, attitudes, intentions, and behaviors that make up the Theory of Reasoned Action[119].

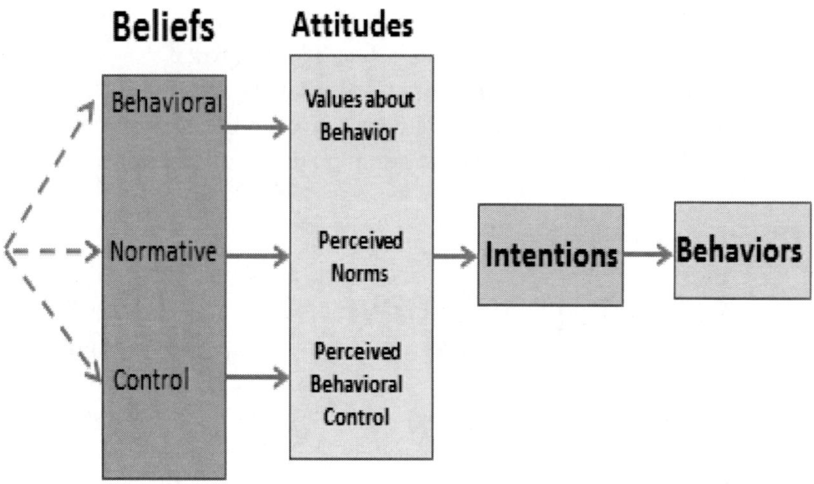

Each person's cognitive beliefs form the basis for their feelings or attitudes. Decisions about commitment are identified in terms of whether the behaviors associated with the expected performance are within their ability to control or accomplish and whether those desired behaviors are socially and normatively acceptable[120].

Those cognitive beliefs affect attitudes that correspond directly with the beliefs and, in turn, impact an individual's intention to make and honor a commitment[121]. Intentions are the best predictors of behaviors, although intervening factors can make completing a commitment difficult[122]. Ultimately, the decisions that each person makes as part of any commitment are derived from their thoughts, which in turn determine their attitudes, intentions, and actions or behaviors[123].

---

[119] Fishbein, M. & Ajzek, I., (2015). *Predicting and Changing Behavior: The Reasoned Action Approach*. New York: Psychology Press.
[120] *Ibid.*
[121] *Ibid.*
[122] *Ibid.*
[123] *Ibid.*

Ultimately, the decisions that each person makes as part of any commitment are derived from their thoughts, which in turn determine their attitudes, intentions, and actions or behaviors.

The individual identity is also affected by the broad beliefs that a person has about her or his self, significant others, the beliefs held about natural laws, experiences from the past, current reality, and beliefs about the future[124]. Any of a multitude of factors can be associated with these core beliefs and these beliefs largely determine the nature of the identity and frame relationships which are the basis for commitments made. The central elements of the identity are the conscious and unconscious ethically-related factors which identify duties owed to others. Those factors directly affect the degree to which individuals feel responsible for honoring commitments made – even without consciously being aware of the impact of the identity on those commitments[125].

The central elements of the identity are the conscious and unconscious ethically-related factors which identify duties owed to others. Those factors directly affect the degree to which individuals feel responsible for honoring commitments made – even without consciously being aware of the impact of the identity on those commitments.

THE IDENTITY

---

[124] Caldwell, C., (2020). "Communication, Meaning, and Identity: Introduction and Overview." In C. Caldwell (Ed.), *Communication, Meaning, and Identity: Moving Toward Discovery.* Hauppauge. NY: NOVA Publishing, Chapter 1.

[125] Burke, P. J. & Stets, J. E., (2009). *Identity Theory*. Oxford, UK: Oxford University Press.

By understanding the nature of their own identity each individual can become much clearer about how (s)he makes decisions, honors commitments or chooses to perform or underperform in keeping promises, and how personal history and life experiences subtly influence their willingness to honor obligations. Factors ranging from the inclination to trust others, the willingness to risk, the obstacles associated with keeping a promise, and a positive or negative view about the world can substantially impact beliefs, attitudes, and intentions associated with honoring commitments[126].

Factors ranging from the **inclination to trust others**, the **willingness to risk**, the **obstacles associated** with **keeping a promise**, and a **positive or negative view about the world** can **substantially impact beliefs, attitudes, and intentions** associated with **honoring commitments**.

Encouragement for Leaders

Being a leader in the 21st Century is a difficult challenge as the worldwide economy and the demand to be more competitive impact the work climate. As leaders pay close attention to how they make commitments and promises, they have the opportunity to increase their understanding of the complex factors that affect their actions. Paying close attention to their own personal histories and identities can help those leaders be more self-aware and improve their ability to avoid overlooking the natural tendency to rationalize decisions about commitments and obligations.

[126] Burke, P. J. & Stets, J. E., (2009), *op. cit.*

As leaders pay close attention to how they make commitments and promises, they have the opportunity to increase their understanding of the complex factors that affect their actions.

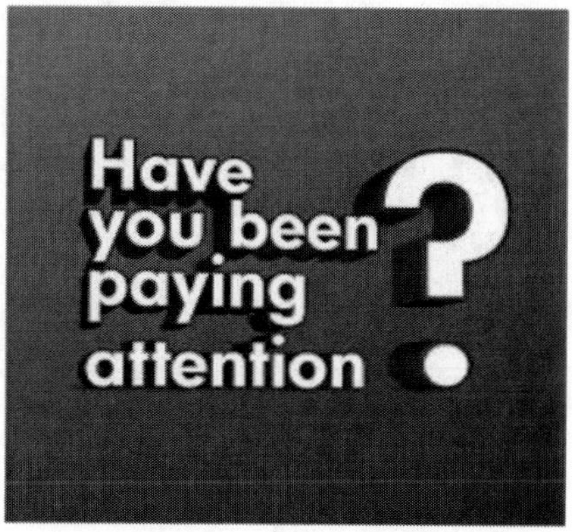

Leading with commitment enables those who lead to establish relationships of high trust and enhances the ability of leaders to retain the followership and engagement that is so necessary for success in today's difficult work climate[127]. By paying close attention to promises made to employees and by honoring relationships, leaders and managers can not only build better relationships but can improve the productivity and effectiveness of their companies. Honoring commitments in their own personal lives can also enable those same leaders and managers to maintain effective relationships outside of the work environment and make their lives more satisfying as well.

Honoring commitments in their own personal lives can also enable those same leaders and managers to maintain effective relationships outside of the work environment and make their lives more satisfying as well.

[127] Clifton, J. & Harter, J., (2019). *It's the Manager*. Omaha, NE: Gallup Press.

References

Burke, P. J. & Stets, J. E., (2009). *Identity Theory*. Oxford, UK: Oxford University Press.

Caldwell, C. & Anderson, V., (2021). "Moral Identity and Core Beliefs." In C. Caldwell & V. Anderson (Eds.). *Moral Identity and Self-Discovery*. Hauppauge, NY: NOVA Publishing, Chapter 3.

Caldwell, C. (2009). "Identity, Self-Deception, and Self-Awareness: Ethical Implications for Leaders and Organizations." *Journal of Business Ethics*, Vol. 90, Supp. 3, pp. 393-406.

Caldwell, C., (2020). "Communication, Meaning, and Identity: Introduction and Overview." In C. Caldwell (Ed.), *Communication, Meaning, and Identity: Moving Toward Discovery*. Hauppauge. NY: NOVA Publishing, Chapter 1.

Catano, V. M., Pond, M. and Kelloway, E. K., (2001), "Exploring Commitment and Leadership in Volunteer Organizations," *Leadership & Organization Development Journal*, Vol. 22 No. 6, pp. 256-263.

Clifton, J. & Harter, J., (2019). *It's the Manager*. Omaha, NE: Gallup Press.

Dethmer, J., Chapman, D. & Klemp, K. W., (2015). *The 15 Commitments of Conscious Leadership: A New Paradigm for Sustainable Success*. Muncie, IN: The Conscious Leadership Group.

Fishbein, M. & Ajzek, I., (2015). *Predicting and Changing Behavior: The Reasoned Action Approach*. New York: Psychology Press.

The Arbinger Institute, (2020). *The Anatomy of Peace: Resolving the Heart of Conflict* (3rd ed.). Oakland, CA: Berrett-Koehler Publishers.

Vroom, V. H., (1994). *Work and Motivation*. San Francisco, CA: Jossey-Bass.

Chapter 4

Passion, Humility, and Fierce Resolve

Although humility may be thought of by some as self-effacing behavior that reflects a low opinion of oneself or personal weakness[128], other experts view humility as a virtuous and vitally important quality of leaders[129]. In his landmark book about companies that achieved greatness, Jim Collins explained that those top companies inevitably were led by leaders who combined personal humility with a fierce resolve[130]. Leaders who lead with great humility, Collins explained, have a correct understanding of themselves, their roles, and the importance of others – and are totally dedicated to excellence in the pursuit of the best possible outcomes for their organizations.

Leaders who lead with great humility have a **correct understanding of themselves, their roles, and the importance of others**– and are **totally dedicated to excellence** in the **pursuit of the best possible outcomes** for their organizations.

The focus of this chapter is on the importance of understanding humility as a quality that motivates leaders to achieve not only outstanding results but

---

[128] Schaffner, A. K., (2021). "What is Humility? The Power of Humility with 5 Practical Exercises." *Positive Psychology*, April 15, 2021 and found online on October 4, 2021 at What is Humility? The Power of Humility with 5 Practical Exercises (positivepsychology.com).

[129] Collins, J., (2001). *Good to Great: Why Some Companies Make the Leap . . . And Others Don't.* New York: Harper Collins.

[130] *Ibid.*

continuous improvement in partnership with others. The chapter begins by defining humility as a leadership perspective that incorporates great commitment and a passion for excellence. The chapter offers ten recommendations for leaders as they interact with others and concludes with a challenge to leaders to incorporate humility in their relationships.

Defining Humility

As an emotional response that drives personal action, humility begins with a cognitive perspective that is based upon perceptions about the world[131]. It is an openness to new ideas and a commitment to partnering with others to achieve excellence[132]. Humility has been defined as the ability "to think rightly of ourselves" – a definition first expressed by the minister, Charles Haddon Spurgeon in 1856[133].

Humility has been defined as **the ability "to think rightly of ourselves"** – a definition first expressed by the minister, **Charles Haddon Spurgeon** in 1856.

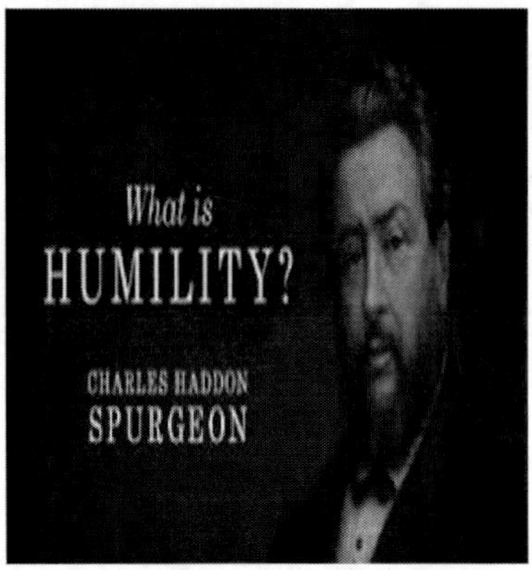

Humility consists of eight meaningful components that enhance self-knowledge and affirm one's identity. As noted by Jim Collins in his landmark book, *Good to Great*, humility consists of the following qualities.

---

[131] Castillo, B. (2008). *Self-Coaching 101: Use Your Mind -- Don't Let It Use You.* Fayetteville, NC: Futures Unlimited Coaching.

[132] Cherry, H., (2021). "What is Humility?" Charles Koch Institute. August 4, 2021 and found online on October 8, 2021 at What is humility? - Charles Koch Institute.

[133] Spurgeon, C. H., (1856). "Pride and Humility." Delivered on August 17, 1856, New Park Street Chapel, Southwark, London, UK.

Self-Understanding

The ability to appreciate and to value oneself, while also acknowledging one's warts and imperfections, is a fundamental condition of humility and is necessary to interact with others and be emotionally healthy[134]. Secretary General of the United Nations, Dag Hammarskjold, explained that humility was neither self-abasement or self-exaltation but was the ability to see oneself accurately and to appreciate one's innate worth[135].

The ability to appreciate and to value oneself, while also acknowledging one's warts and imperfections, is a fundamental condition of humility and is necessary to interact with others and be emotionally healthy.

Valuing Others

In recognizing their own value, individuals with humility also appreciate that others also possess almost limitless potential. Wise leaders willingly acknowledge the capabilities of others, choose individuals with which to work who complement their own talents and have no difficulty in recognizing that others may possess abilities and talents that are greater than their own[136].

---

134 Fromm, E., (2006). *The Art of Loving*. New York: Harper Perennial.
135 Sjoberg, L. & Auden, W. H., (1965). *Dag Hammarskjold – Markings*. New York: Alfred A. Knopf Publishing.
136 Collins, J., (2001), *op. cit.*

Wise leaders **willingly acknowledge the capabilities of others, choose individuals** with which to work **who complement their own talents.** and **have no difficulty in recognizing** that **others may possess abilities and talents that are greater than their own.**

Passionate Commitment

Driven by their own commitment to become their best version of themselves and their commitment to others, humility creates in leaders a passionate desire to excel, to learn, and to give their best effort to the goals that they pursue[137]. The fierce resolve of humility drives great leaders to recognize that "good is the enemy of great[138]" and to not be satisfied with "good enough."

Driven by their own commitment to become their **best version of themselves** and **their commitment to others, humility creates in leaders a passionate desire** to **excel,** to **learn**, and to **give their best effort** to the **goals that they pursue**.

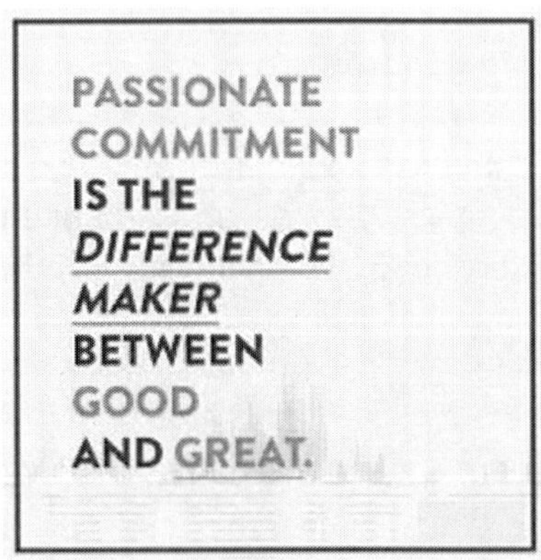

[137] *Ibid.*
[138] *Ibid.*, p. 1.

Giving Credit

The willingness to give others credit for successes recognizes the importance of shared efforts in contributing to an organization's accomplishments[139]. Valuing the vital importance of interdependence and collaboration acknowledges that outcomes are rarely achieved by any single individual. This ability to "look out the window" when great achievements occur – willingly sharing credit for success – reflects the leader's ability to understand the realities of achievement[140].

Valuing the vital importance of interdependence and collaboration acknowledges that outcomes are rarely achieved by any single individual.

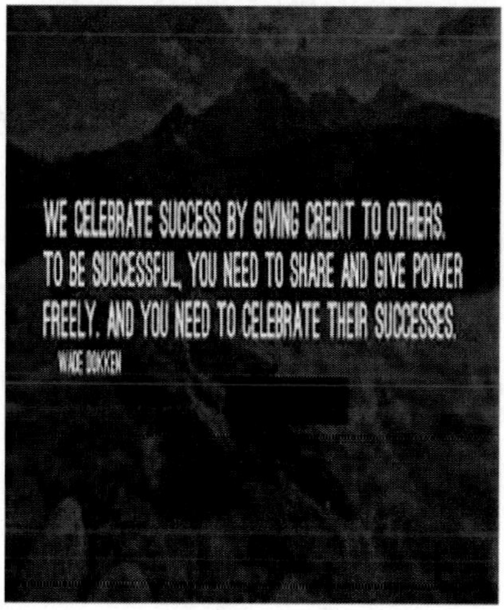

Accepting Responsibility

Leaders with humility take full ownership for mistakes that are made by those who work "on their watch." Although they acknowledge the accomplishments of the organization as a team achievement, leaders with humility take personal accountability for their company's shortcomings. They never blame others but "look in the mirror" in accepting their responsibility for any missteps or failures.

---

139 *Ibid.*

140 Collins, J., (2001). "Level 5 Leadership: The Triumph of Humility and Fierce Resolve." *Harvard Business Review*, January 1, 2001 and found online on October 5, 2001 at Level 5 Leadership: The Triumph of Humility and Fierce Resolve (hbr.org).

Although they acknowledge the **accomplishments** of the organization **as a team achievement, leaders with humility** take **personal accountability** for **their company's shortcomings.**

Compelling Modesty

Humble leaders are not self-seeking or focused on their own image in the world. Leaders with humility quietly and determinedly go about their work with the intended goal of achieving their mission and purpose, rather than promoting themselves. Their modesty seeks to focus the efforts in which they are engaged on accomplishing their organization's priorities, rather than on personally looking good[141].

Leaders with humility quietly and determinedly go about their work with the intended **goal of achieving their mission and purpose**, rather than **promoting themselves.**

[141] *Ibid.*

Standards Driven

The underlying motivation of leaders who possess humility is that they possess a highly developed set of moral standards that serve as the foundation for their actions. These standards acknowledge the leader's obligation to be ethical stewards that serve the needs of all of the stakeholders associated with an organization. Driven by these standards, leaders with humility willingly set an example by incorporating those standards in their daily interactions.

The **underlying motivation** of **leaders who possess humility** is a **highly developed set of moral standards** that serve as **the foundation for their actions.**

Constantly Learning

Humility drives those who possess it to constantly improve, to seek new insights, and to better themselves so that they can honor their obligations to those with whom they work, to society, and to themselves[142]. Learning and applying that which they learn makes it possible for humble leaders to achieve outcomes that others may not recognize as reachable and enables individuals and organizations to accomplish results that may startle others.

---

[142] Owens, B. P. & Hekman, D. R., (2012). "Modeling How to Grow: An Inductive Examination of Humble Leader Behaviors, Contingencies, and Outcomes." *Academy of Management Review*, Vol. 55, No. 4, pp. 787-818.

Learning and applying that which they learn makes it possible for humble leaders to achieve outcomes that others may not recognize as reachable and enables individuals and organizations to accomplish results that may startle others.

Each of these qualities that define humility enables leaders to earn the trust and respect of others and serve as examples that inspire, motivate, and encourage others to become their best selves and to follow a leader's example[143]. Humility's virtues enable leaders to set a personal example that helps their colleagues to appreciate their leader's commitment to the organization and their respect for others.

Humility's virtues enable leaders to set a personal example that helps their colleagues to appreciate their leader's commitment to the organization and their respect for others.

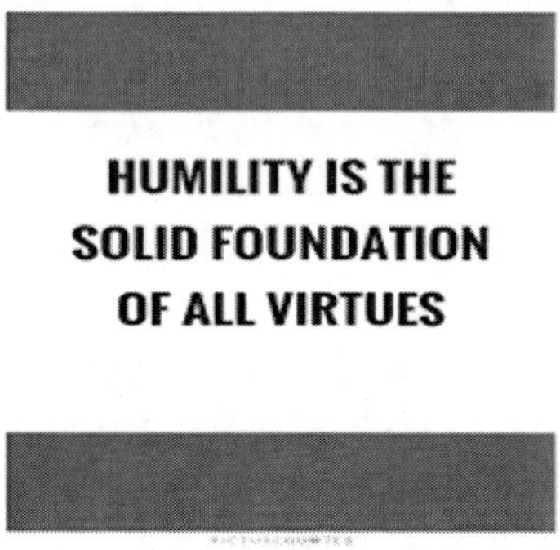

[143] Owens, B. P., (2009). *Humility in Organizational Leadership*. Seattle, WA: University of Washington Press.

Ten Recommendations

As those who wish to lead others reflect on Collins' insights about the importance of humility, those individuals would be well served to understand the important role that humility plays in human relationships. Consistent with that role, those who have written about humility and leadership provide wisdom that can be incorporated into ten recommendations.

1) Invest in Personal Self-Discovery about Your Identity

The self-understanding that is so vital in humility is achieved by making an in-depth commitment to understand oneself[144]. One's identity is often subconsciously formed and the values upon which the identity is based are typically rarely understood at the conscious level on a day-to-day basis[145]. As individuals become more self-aware by investing in personal self-discovery, they acquire the ability to understand themselves and appreciate the importance of aligning their actions with consciously chosen values[146]. That personal awareness is critical to the process of self-understanding, emotional intelligence, and humility[147].

As individuals become more self-aware by investing in personal self-discovery, they acquire the ability to understand themselves and appreciate the importance of aligning their actions with consciously chosen values.

---

[144] Caldwell, C. & Anderson, V. (2019). "Humility and Personal Progress: Insights about Identity" in Anderson, V. & Caldwell, C., (Eds.), *Humility as Enlightened Leadership*. Hauppauge, NY: NOVA Publishers, Chapter 3.

[145] Burke, P. J. & Stets, J. E., (2009). *Identity Theory*. Oxford, UK: Oxford University Press.

[146] *Ibid.*

[147] Caldwell, C., (2020). "Acquiring Meaning through Self-Understanding." *Communication, Meaning, and Identity: Moving Toward Discovery*. Hauppauge, NY: NOVA Publishing, Chapter 6.

2) Build Interpersonal Relationships based upon Mutual Respect

The leadership author, Ken Blanchard has advised "Don't think less of yourself, just think of yourself less[148]." When leaders demonstrate that they care genuinely about others and treat them with great respect, they are perceived as both more ethical and more authentic[149]. Leaders who adopt humility's respect for others and commitment to their welfare demonstrate leadership that honors the leader's obligation to serve others that Max DePree called a "covenantal duty[150]." The Swiss philosopher, Henri Frederic Amiel declared that "There is no respect for others without humility in oneself[151]."

When leaders demonstrate that they care genuinely about others and treat those with whom they work with great respect, they are perceived as both more ethical and more authentic.

3) Conduct Oneself with Integrity in Every Action

Humility and integrity are inseparable virtues. Integrity and humility both constitute purity of intent, character, and action[152]. Without integrity a leader is perceived as unworthy of being trusted. Humility is the means by which

---

[148] Blanchard, K., (1990). *Democrat and Chronicle* cited in Shakohl, T., (2019). "Fact Check: Did C. S. Lewis Say, 'Humility Isn't Thinking Less of Yourself – It's Thinking of Yourself Less'?" found online on October 8, 2021 at FACT CHECK: Did CS Lewis Say, 'Humility Isn't Thinking Less of Yourself – It's Thinking of Yourself Less'? | Check Your Fact.

[149] See George, B., (2004). *Authentic Leadership: Rediscovering the Secrets to Creating Lasting Value*. San Francisco, CA: Jossey-Bass and Atwijuka, S., & Caldwell, C., (2017). "Authentic Leadership and the Ethic of Care." *Journal of Management Development*, Vol. 36, Iss. 8, pp. 1040.

[150] DePree, M., (2004). *Leadership is an Art*. New York: Crown Publishing, Chapter 1.

[151] Amiel, H. F. & Ward, H., (2012). *Amiel's Journal*. Charleston, SC: BiblioLife Publishers.

[152] Bauman, D. C., (2013). "Leadership and the Three Face of Integrity." *The Leadership Quarterly*, Vol. 24, Iss. 3, pp. 414-426.

every leader honors his or her moral duties to others[153]. Integrity and humility are both based upon a foundation of love for self and for others[154].

Without integrity a leader is perceived as **unworthy of being trusted** and **humility is the means** by which **every leader honors** his or her **moral duties** to others.

4) Empower Others to Demonstrate Your Trust

Humility is demonstrated by empowering others and demonstrates that a leader recognizes the competence and ability of those who are trusted. To empower others is to honor their role and to acknowledge their capability to perform important tasks. Trusting and empowering others creates trust in return[155]. Empowering includes developing and training others, rather than simply delegating responsibility or asking others to be accountable.

---

[153] Mayer, R. C., Davis, J. H., & Schoorman, F. D., (1995). "An Integrative Model of Organizational Trust." *Academy of Management Review*. Vol 20, No. 3, pp. 709-734.

[154] Pulsifer, B., "75 Quotes on Integrity" found online on October 8, 2021 at 75 Quotes on Integrity | Inspiring Workspaces by BOS.

[155] Kouzes, J. M. & Posner, B. Z., (2011). *Credibility: How Leaders Gain and Lose It, Why People Demand It*. San Francisco, CA: Jossey-Bass.

To empower others is to **honor their role** and to **acknowledge their capability** to **perform important tasks.**

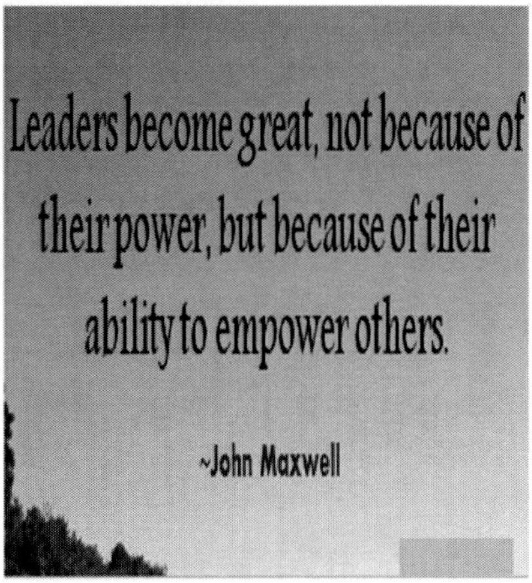

5) Seek to "Do Right," Rather than to "Be Right"

"Being right" is often motivated by t how we wish to be perceived by others. "Doing right" requires that our actions fit the context of a situation, the needs of others, and the duties and obligations that we owe. It takes character, mental and spiritual toughness, and a commitment to honoring the truth to do what is right in a world where choices can be difficult and temptations are great. The challenge to do what is right is the challenge to live a life of virtue. Doing what is right is because it is the right thing to do – not because it leads to a personal benefit[156].

It takes **character, mental and spiritual toughness,** and a **commitment to honoring the truth** to **do what is right** in a **world** where **choices can be difficult** and **temptations are great.**

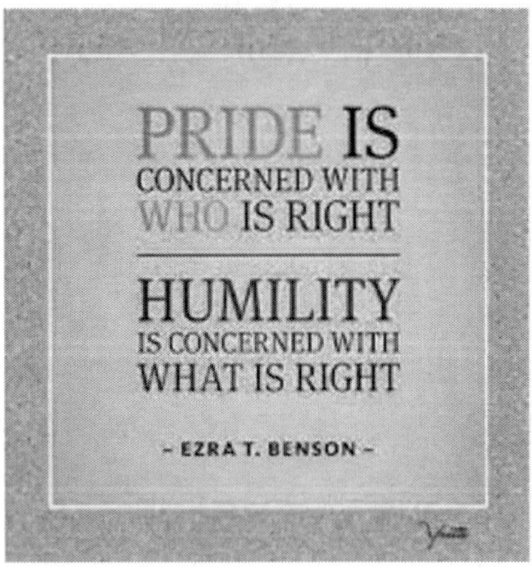

[156] Aurelius, M., (2019). *Meditations*. New York: SDE Book Publishers, Book 5.

6) Listen to Others and Make Them Full Partners

The British best-selling author, Simon Sinek, reminds us that "Humility is being open to the ideas of others[157]." By making others full owners and partners and by listening to their input, leaders create shared commitment[158]. Those who lead in this manner merit others' trust and demonstrate their moral obligation to those whom they lead[159]. Mary Parker Follett was a strong advocate of enabling and empowering others as partners and decision-makers and emphasized that sharing responsibility made leaders and organizations stronger[160].

By making others full owners and partners and by listening to their input, leaders create shared commitment. Those who lead in this manner merit others' trust and demonstrate their moral obligation to those whom they lead.

7) Give Full Credit to Others for Their Achievements

Taking credit for the achievements of others destroys trust and is the antithesis of humility[161]. Acknowledging the great contributions that others make in achieving an organization's goals gives individuals and teams the credit that they rightly deserve, builds their sense of organization commitment, and inspires greater efforts[162]. Claiming credit for the efforts of othersundermines goodwill and destroys trust[163].

---

[157] Sinek, S., (2011). *Start with Why: How Great Leaders Inspire Everyone to Take Action*. New York: Portfolio.

[158] Block, P., (2013). *Stewardship: Choosing Service Over Self-Interest*. San Francisco: Jossey-Bass.

[159] *Ibid.*

[160] Follett, M. P., (2013). *Dynamic Administration: The Collected Papers of Mary Parker Follett*. Eastford, CT: Martino Fine Books.

[161] Collins, J., (2001), *op. cit.*

[162] Luthans, K, (2000). "Recognition: A Powerful, but often Overlooked, Leadership Tool to Improve Employee Performance." *Journal of Leadership and Organizational Studies*, Vol. 7, Iss. 1, pp. 31-39.

[163] Quast, L, (2012). "When a Boss Takes Credit for Your Work." *Forbes*, July 9, 2012 and found online on October 8, 2021 at When A Boss Takes Credit For Your Work (forbes.com).

Acknowledging the great contributions that others make in achieving an organization's goals gives individuals and teams the credit that they rightly deserve, builds their sense of organization commitment, and inspires greater efforts.

Share The Credit

8) Strive to Constantly Learn and be Teachable

Michael Josephson, a widely respected expert about ethics and leadership, explained that "wisdom requires both courage and humility to consider new facts, opinions, and perspectives even when they challenge long and deeply held beliefs[164]." Humility is being teachable even when one is considered an expert. The willingness to constantly learn and the commitment to constant improvement are fundamental elements of humility that enable leaders to not only set an example but to motivate others to also seek to grow[165].

The willingness to constantly learn and the commitment to constant improvement are fundamental elements of humility that enable leaders to not only set an example but to motivate others to also seek to grow.

---

[164] Josephson, M., (2016). "Commentary: Intellectual Humility and the Pursuit of Wisdom. 'Don't Believe Everything You Think.'" *Whatwillmatter.com* found online on October 8, 2021 at Commentary: INTELLECTUAL HUMILITY AND THE PURSUIT OF WISDOM. "Don't believe everything you think." | What Will Matter.

[165] Owens, B. P. & Hekman, D. R., (2012), *op. cit.*

9) Adopt the Principles of Servant Leadership

Leaders with humility view their obligation to serve others as a moral responsibility owed to each individual and to the organization[166]. Leaders who adopt a servant leadership philosophy view service to others as their first obligation and put service to others above their own self-interest[167]. Servant leaders empower their colleagues with value and purpose, enabling them to achieve their potential in the process of achieving their organization's goals[168].

Leaders who adopt servant leadership view service to others as their first obligation and put service to others above their own self-interest.

10) Constantly Evaluate and Polish Your Personal Progress

Assessing personal progress is critical to sustaining growth and to aligning one's actions with values[169]. A key to honoring one's identity is to convert the values that one adopts into specific actions and outcomes[170]. The understanding of how actions reflect personal beliefs requires monitoring those actions, examining intent, and identifying and honoring duties owed[171]. The process of personal progress demands consistent reflection and a commitment to the ideals and values upon which integrity is based[172].

---

[166] DePree, M., (2004), *op. cit.*

[167] Block, P., (2013), *op. cit.*

[168] Greenleaf, R. K., (2002). *Servant Leadership: A Journey into the Nature of Legitimate Power and Greatness 25th Anniversary Edition*. Mahwah, NJ: Paulist Press.

[169] Aurelius, M., (2019), *op. cit.*, Book 6.

[170] Caldwell, C. & Anderson, V., (2021). "Moral Identity, Self-Improvement, and the Quest for Greatness: A Leadership Responsibility." *Journal of Values-Based Leadership*, Vol. 14, Iss. 2, Article 4 found online at Moral Identity, Self-Improvement, and the Quest for Greatness: A Leadership Responsibility (valpo.edu).

[171] Burke, P. J. & Stets, J. E., (2009), *op. cit.*

[172] Caldwell, C. & Anderson, V., (2021). "Moral Identity and Finding Your Voice" in C. Caldwell & V. Anderson (Eds.). *Moral Identity and Self-Discovery*. Hauppauge, NY: NOVA Publishers, Chapter 2.

The understanding of how actions reflect personal beliefs requires monitoring those actions, examining intent, and identifying and honoring duties owed.

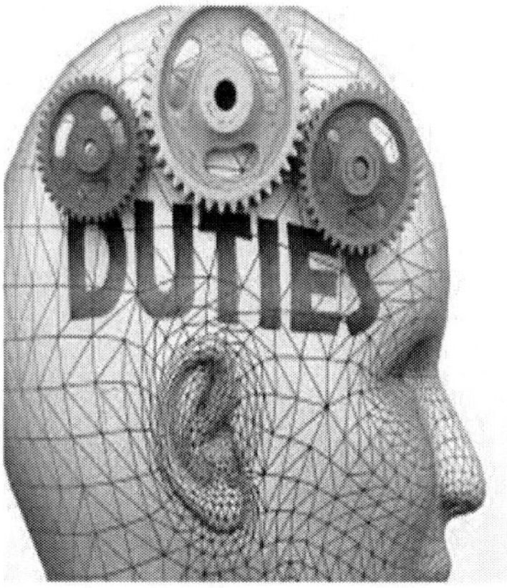

By following these ten recommendations, those who lead can enhance their ability to adopt the qualities of humility and strengthen their capacity to dedicate themselves to personal and organizational excellence.

The Challenge to Leaders

Those who lead, and those who wish to lead more effectively, often struggle as they seek to enhance their ability to earn the trust and commitment of others[173]. It is well established that leaders who model the qualities of leadership are much more successful in obtaining others' respect and followership[174]. A growing body of evidence confirms that leaders who develop the qualities of humility and fierce resolve to achieve excellence are far more successful than their peers in leading their organizations[175].

By understanding the nature of humility and incorporating the ten recommendations suggested in this chapter, those who lead can not only refine their personal character but can enhance their ability to lead. Humility's virtues enable those who acquire it to dedicate themselves more fully to personal excellence. By becoming the best versions of themselves, leaders

---

[173] Collins, J., (2001), *op. cit.*

[174] Kouzes, J. M. & Posner, B.Z., (2017). *The Leadership Challenge: How to Make Extraordinary Things Happen in Organizations* (7th ed.). San Francisco, CA: Jossey-Bass, Chapter 4.

[175] Collins, J., (2001), *op. cit.*

with humility establish those same standards for others and are more likely to see others respond with that same commitment and passion[176].

A growing body of evidence confirms that leaders who develop the qualities of humility and fierce resolve are far more successful than their peers in leading their organizations.

By becoming the best versions of themselves leaders with humility establish those same standards for others and are more likely to see others respond with that same commitment and passion

References

Amiel, H. F. & Ward, H., (2012). *Amiel's Journal*. Charleston, SC: BiblioLife Publishers.
Atwijuka, S., & Caldwell, C., (2017). "Authentic Leadership and the Ethic of Care." *Journal of Management Development*, Vol. 36, Iss. 8, pp. 1040.
Aurelius, M., (2019). *Meditations*. New York: SDE Book Publishers, Book 5.

[176] Owens, B. P. & Hekman, D. R., (2012), *op. cit.*

Bauman, D. C., (2013). "Leadership and the Three Face of Integrity." *The Leadership Quarterly*, Vol. 24, Iss. 3, pp. 414-426.

Blanchard, K., (1990). *Democrat and Chronicle* cited in Shakohl, T., (2019). "Fact Check: Did C. S. Lewis Say, 'Humility Isn't Thinking Less of Yourself – It's Thinking of Yourself Less'?" found online on October 8, 2021 at FACT CHECK: Did CS Lewis Say, 'Humility Isn't Thinking Less Of Yourself – It's Thinking Of Yourself Less'? | Check Your Fact.

Block, P., (2013). *Stewardship: Choosing Service Over Self-Interest.* San Francisco: Jossey-Bass.

Burke, P. J. & Stets, J. E., (2009). *Identity Theory*. Oxford, UK: Oxford University Press.

Caldwell, C., (2020). "Acquiring Meaning through Self-Understanding." *Communication, Meaning, and Identity: Moving Toward Discovery*. Hauppauge, NY: NOVA Publishing, Chapter 6.

Caldwell, C. & Anderson, V., (2021). "Moral Identity, Self-Improvement, and the Quest for Greatness: A Leadership Responsibility." *Journal of Values-Based Leadership*, Vol. 14, Iss. 2, Article 4 found online at Moral Identity, Self-Improvement, and the Quest for Greatness: A Leadership Responsibility (valpo.edu).

Caldwell, C. & Anderson, V., (2021). "Moral Identity and Finding Your Voice" in C. Caldwell & V. Anderson (Eds.). *Moral Identity and Self-Discovery*. Hauppauge, NY: NOVA Publishers, Chapter 2.

Caldwell, C. & Anderson, V. (2019). "Humility and Personal Progress: Insights about Identity" in Anderson, V. & Caldwell, C., (Eds.), *Humility as Enlightened Leadership*. Hauppauge, NY: NOVA Publishers, Chapter 3.

Castillo, B. (2008). *Self-Coaching 101: Use Your Mind – Don't Let It Use You*. Fayetteville, NC: Futures Unlimited Coaching.

Cherry, H., (2021). "What is Humility?" Charles Koch Institute. August 4, 2021 and found online on October 8, 2021 at What is humility? - Charles Koch Institute.

Collins, J., (2001). *Good to Great: Why Some Companies Make the Leap . . . And Others Don't*. New York: Harper Collins.

Collins, J., (2001). "Level 5 Leadership: The Triumph of Humility and Fierce Resolve." *Harvard Business Review*, January 1, 2001 and found online on October 5, 2001 at Level 5 Leadership: The Triumph of Humility and Fierce Resolve (hbr.org).

DePree, M., (2004). *Leadership is an Art*. New York: Crown Publishing, Chapter 1.

Follett, M. P., (2013). *Dynamic Administration: The Collected Papers of Mary Parker Follett*. Eastford, CT: Martino Fine Books.

Fromm, E., (2006). *The Art of Loving*. New York: Harper Perennial.

George, B., (2004). *Authentic Leadership: Rediscovering the Secrets to Creating Lasting Value*. San Francisco, CA: Jossey-Bass.

Greenleaf, R. K., (2002). *Servant Leadership: A Journey into the Nature of Legitimate Power and Greatness 25th Anniversary Edition*. Mahwah, NJ: Paulist Press.

Josephson, M., (2016). "Commentary: Intellectual Humility and the Pursuit of Wisdom. 'Don't Believe Everything You Think.'" *Whatwillmatter.com* found online on October 8, 2021 at Commentary: Intellectual Humility and the Pursuit Of Wisdom. "Don't believe everything you think." | What Will Matter.

Kouzes, J. M. & Posner, B.Z., (2017). *The Leadership Challenge: How to Make Extraordinary Things Happen in Organizations* (7th ed.). San Francisco, CA: Jossey-Bass, Chapter 4.

Kouzes, J. M. & Posner, B. Z., (2011). *Credibility: How Leaders Gain and Lose It, Why People Demand It.* San Francisco, CA: Jossey-Bass.

Luthans, K, (2000). "Recognition: A Powerful, but often Overlooked, Leadership Tool to Improve Employee Performance." *Journal of Leadership and Organizational Studies*, Vol. 7, Iss. 1, pp. 31-39Mayer, R. C., Davis, J. H., & Schoorman, F. D., (1995). "An Integrative Model of Organizational Trust." *Academy of Management Review*. Vol 20, No. 3, pp. 709-734.

Owens, B. P. & Hekman, D. R., (2012). "Modeling How to Grow: An Inductive Examination of Humble Leader Behaviors, Contingencies, and Outcomes." *Academy of Management Review*, Vol. 55, No. 4, pp. 787-818.

Owens, B. P., (2009). *Humility in Organizational Leadership.* Seattle, WA: University of Washington Press.

Pulsifer, B., "75 Quotes on Integrity" found online on October 8, 2021 at 75 Quotes on Integrity | Inspiring Workspaces by BOS.

Quast, L, (2012). "When a Boss Takes Credit for Your Work." *Forbes*, July 9, 2012 and found online on October 8, 2021 at When A Boss Takes Credit For Your Work (forbes.com).

Schaffner, A. K., (2021). "What is Humility? The Power of Humility with 5 Practical Exercises." *Positive Psychology*, April 15, 2021 and found online on October 4, 2021 at What is Humility? The Power Of Humility with 5 Practical Exercises (positivepsychology.com).

Sinek, S., (2011). *Start with Why: How Great Leaders Inspire Everyone to Take Action.* New York: Portfolio.

Sjoberg, L. & Auden, W. H., (1965). *Dag Hammarskjold – Markings*. New York: Alfred A. Knopf Publishing.

Spurgeon, C. H., (1856). "Pride and Humility." Delivered on August 17, 1856, New Park Street Chapel, Southwark, London, UK.

Chapter 5

Persistence, Perseverance, and Character – The Power of Commitment

In his highly regarded book about the importance of becoming one's best self, Harvard University's Clayton M. Christensen and colleagues posed the powerful question, "How will you measure your life?[177]" The answer to that question is ultimately achieved by determining the standards and principles by which one will govern life's decisions and then having the personal integrity and commitment to live each day consistent with those guidelines.

"How will you measure your life?" The answer to that question is ultimately achieved by **determining the standards and principles** by which one will govern life's decisions and **having the personal integrity and commitment to live each day consistent with those guidelines**.

How Will You Measure Your Life?

Clayton M. Christensen

This power of integrity and commitment is based upon each person's persistence, perseverance, and character – the focus upon which this chapter is based. We begin this chapter by distinguishing the differences between persistence and perseverance and their relationship to personal character. Following that introduction, we examine seven characteristics that lead to perseverance and that contribute to a leader's ability to demonstrate her/his personal character and integrity. The chapter concludes with a challenge to

[177] Christensen, C. M., Allworth, J. & Dillon, K., (2012). *How Will You Measure Your Life?* New York: Harper Business.

leaders to understand the importance of being men and women who persevere as they strive to earn the followership and trust of others.

The Nature of Persistence

Persistence is the personal tenacity, determination, and resolve to pursue a course of action despite difficulties, obstacles, or resistance[178]. As a phenomenon of human behavior, persistence has been studied for more than a century in an attempt to understand the factors that determine personal commitment and resilience[179]. Persistence in attempting to accomplish a desired outcome is sometimes perceived as an irritation and a nuisance to those who may be opposed to the unceasing efforts of another party or as evidence of profound personal courage by those who admire the dedication demonstrated to achieve a desired goal.

As a phenomenon of human behavior, persistence has been studied for more than a century in an attempt to understand the factors that determine personal commitment and resilience.

Aristotle wrote about persistence in reminding the world that persistent effort leads to success[180]. He is attributed to have said that "We are what we

[178] Lufi, D. & Cohen, A., (1987). "A Scale for Measuring Persistence in Children." *Journal of Personality Assessment*, Vol. 51, No. 2, pp. 178-185.

[179] *Ibid.*

[180] Sylvester, B., (2019). "Fact Check: Did Aristotle Say 'We are what we repeatedly do?'" CheckYourFact, June 16, 2019 and found online on October 10, 2021 at FACT CHECK: Did Aristotle Say, 'We Are What We Repeatedly Do'? | Check Your Fact.

repeatedly do. Excellence, then, is not an act but a habit[181]." Similarly, Ralph Waldo Emerson observed that persistence was a key to personal improvement. He wrote, "That which we persist in doing becomes easier to do, not that the nature of the thing has changed but our power to do so has increased[182]."

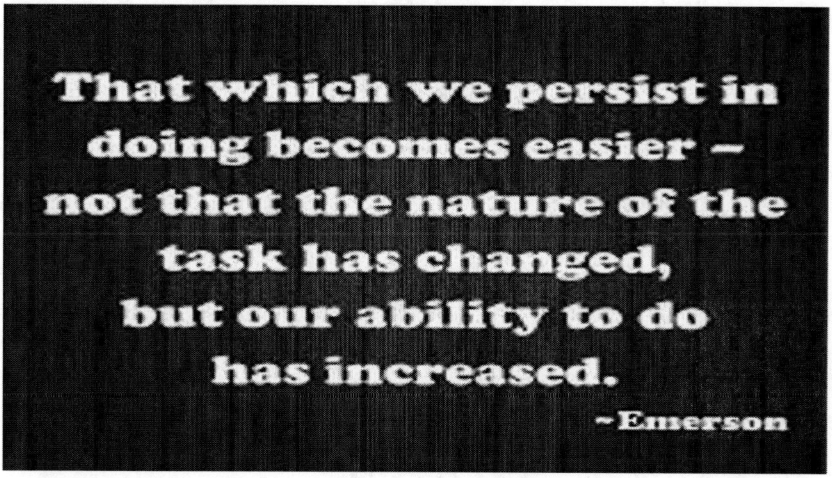

Persistence has been equated with the study of goal achievement and personal motivation. As a concept of behavioral choice, it is often associated with expectancy theory[183], expectations of personal self-efficacy[184], control theory[185], identity theory[186], and the theory of reasoned action[187]. Meier and Albrecht described persistence as a function of three factors or stages[188]:

---

181 *Ibid.*

182 "Ralph Waldo Emerson Quotes." *Goodreads.com*, found online on October 10, 2021 at Quote by Ralph Waldo Emerson: "That which we persist in doing becomes easier t..." (goodreads.com).

183 Vroom, V. (1964). *Work and Motivation*. New York, NY: Wiley and Sons.

184 Bandura, A. (1977). "Self-Efficacy: Toward a Unifying Theory of Behavioral Change." *Psychological Review*, Vol. 84, pp. 191-215.

185 Carver, C.S. (1979). "A Cybernetic Model of Self-Attention Processes." *Journal of Personality and Social Psychology*, Vol. 37, pp. 1251-1281.

186 Burke, P. J. & Stets, J. E., (2009). *Identity Theory*. Oxford, UK: Oxford University Press.

187 Fishbein, M. & Ajzen, I., (2015). *Predicting and Changing Behavior: The Reasoned Action Approach*. New York: Psychology Press.

188 Meier, G. & Albrecht. M. H., (2003). "The Persistence Process: Development of a Stage Model for Goal-Directed Behavior." *Journal of Leadership and Organizational Studies*, Vol. 10, No. 2, pp. 43-54.

1. *A Goal Decision* – A decision is made that a desired objective or outcome is attainable in terms of its ability to accomplish an intended purpose. within one's capability of achieving, and likely to be achieved with the required effort.
2. *Task Acceptance* – Each person identifies the feasibility of a task within her or capability of performing the tasks required to accomplish the goal.
3. *Evaluation* – The process of identifying the likelihood that the desired result will be achievable with the required effort is based upon ongoing progress in accomplishing what is intended and feedback received along the way.

Incremental decisions are made throughout these three stages amd determine an individual's willingness to persist[189]. The stronger the positive evaluation of the likelihood of a desired outcome, the greater is the probability that an individual will persist in the pursuit of that outcome. Thus, persistence is an emotional response based upon the cognitive assessment of the many factors that must be taken into account in assessing the likelihood of achieving a desired goal and purpose[190].

Persistence is an **emotional response** based upon the **cognitive assessment of the many factors** that must be **taken into account in assessing** the **likelihood of achieving a desired goal and purpose.**

[189] *Ibid.*
[190] Fishbein, M. & Ajzen, I., (2015), *op. cit.*

Understanding Perseverance

Perseverance is persistence at a higher level and reflects a willingness to endure and continue to pursue a worthy outcome, despite a delay or unanticipated difficulty that makes the achievement of the goal or purpose less likely to occur with the effort expected. Duckworth and colleagues have suggested that persistence and perseverance can be distinguished based upon the grit, or higher level of commitment and effort, that an individual is willing to exert to achieve a desired result[191].

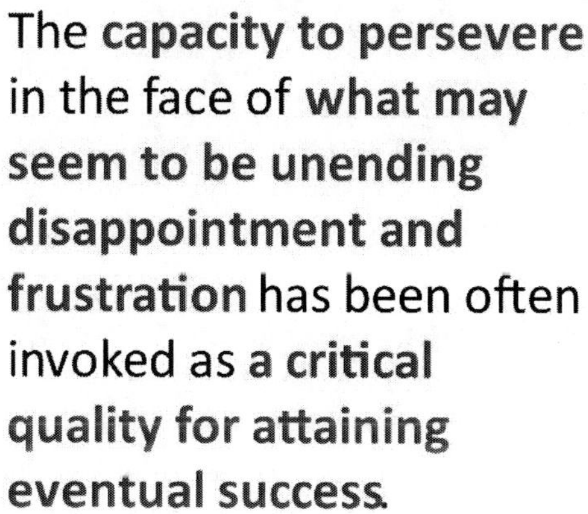

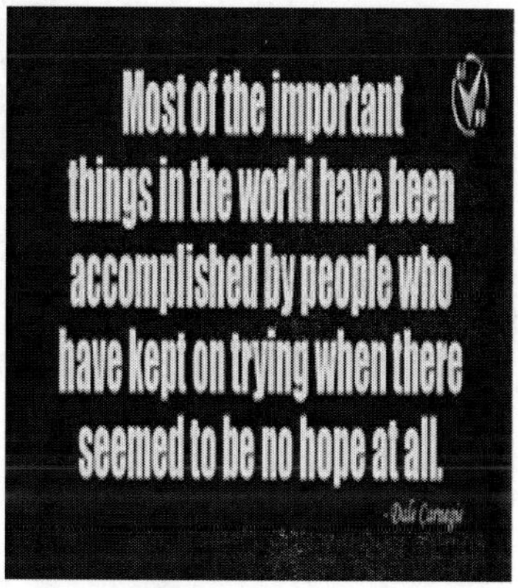

The capacity to persevere in the face of what may seem to be unending disappointment and frustration has been often invoked as a critical quality for attaining eventual success. Perhaps one of the most frequently cited examples of a person with perseverance is Thomas Alva Edison. Edison opined, "Our greatest weakness is in giving up. The most certain way to succeed is to try just one more time[192]." In his quest to create the light bulb, Edison also said, "I have not failed. I've just found 10,000 ways that won't work[193]." But Edison persevered and eventually succeeded.

---

[191] Duckworth, A.L., Peterson, C., Matthews, M.D., & Kelly, D.R. (2007). "Grit: Perseverance and Passion for Long-term Goals." *Journal of Personality and Social Psychology*, Vol. 92, pp. 1087-1101.

[192] "Perseverance Quotes." *AZ Quotes,com* found online on October 10, 2021 at TOP 25 PERSEVERANCE QUOTES (of 1000) | A-Z Quotes (azquotes.com).

[193] "Thomas Edison Quotes." BrainyQuote.com. Found online on October 10, 2021 at Thomas A. Edison - I have not failed. I've just found... (brainyquote.com).

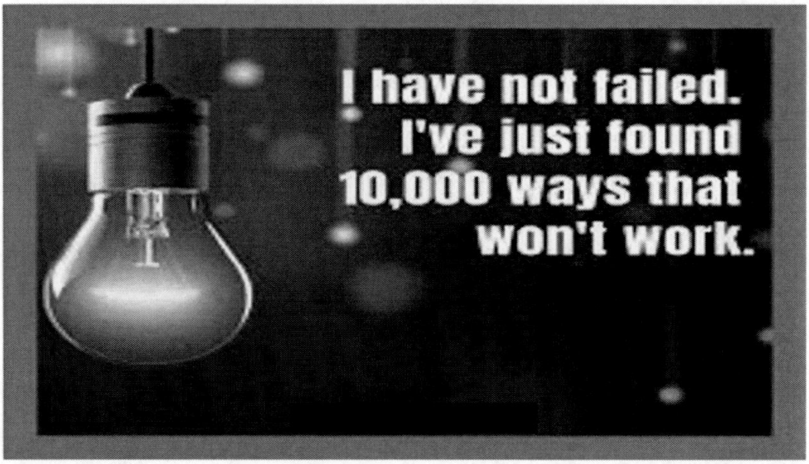

Perseverance reflects a higher level of self-efficacy or personal confidence in one's ability to accomplish a goal than persistence, but it also incorporates a greater moral commitment to the desired outcome and a higher level of personal conscientiousness[194]. The diligence of conscientiousness is derived from the personal obligation to patiently and often painfully endure in making the continuing effort to achieve a goal – even when recognizing that the results will probably come at a future time.

The **differences between persistence and perseverance** are **the degree of personal enthusiasm, dedication, and commitment** to **achieving an outcome** and the **refusal to give up** – despite **facing what seem** to be **daunting and challenging obstacles**.

The Differences between Persistence and Perseverance

[194] Duckworth, A.L., Peterson, C., Matthews, M.D., & Kelly, D.R. (2007), *op. cit.*

The differences between persistence and perseverance are the degree of personal enthusiasm, dedication, and commitment to achieving an outcome and the refusal to give up – despite facing what seem to be daunting and challenging obstacles. Both persistence and perseverance reflect the cognitive belief that one's efforts are worth continuing coupled with a sense of personal responsibility or moral obligation to maintain those efforts. King and Carruthers have noted that moral responsibility and conscious choice are related and the sense of personal duty or obligation is rationally derived and affects the ability to maintain effort[195].

Moral responsibility and conscious choice are related and the sense of personal duty or obligation is rationally derived and affects the ability to maintain effort.

The Contribution of Character

Character is the set of mental and moral qualities distinctive to each individual that determine the pattern of their individual behaviors[196]. The link between character and integrity is often assumed and a person of "good character" is expected to have a high integrity that is demonstrated by honoring commitments, being true to one's standards and beliefs, and dealing honestly with others. The challenge with the integrity gap is "between what we believe

[195] King, M. & Carruthers, P., (2012). "Moral Responsibility and Consciousness." *Journal of Moral Philosophy*, Vol. 9, pp. 200-228.

[196] Kupperman, J., (1995). *Character*. Oxford, UK: Oxford University Press.

and how we behave[197]." Often character is developed by adversity. Albert Einstein explained that "Adversity introduces a man to himself[198]."

Facing the challenges of life teaches a man or woman that what has real value is rarely achieved easily. Martin Luther King, Jr. reminded the world that the ultimate measure of a man or woman is where (s)he stands during times of challenge and controversy[199].

When we combine character with integrity, we not only recognize that conduct is right or wrong, but we make the decision to do what is right – even when that choice may be painful or difficult. Character strengthens resolve and provides the added strength to hang on, to endure, and to be personally dedicated to the achievement of a worthy outcome. Character combined with integrity and commitment sustains persistence and perseverance and ultimately makes it possible to achieve what others often fail to accomplish[200].

---

[197] Stone, B. & Ukleja, M., (2009). *The Ethics Challenge: Strengthening Your Integrity in a Greedy World.* New York: Morgan James Publishing.

[198] Kleckner, J., (2018). "80 Albert Einstein Quotes to Inspire You for Life." Addicted2Success, December 18, 2018 and found online on October 10, 2021 at 80 Albert Einstein Quotes to Inspire You For Life (addicted2success.com),

[199] Martin Luther King, Jr. Quotes. Goodreads.com. Found online on October 10, 2021 at Martin Luther King Jr. Quotes (Author of The Autobiography of Martin Luther King, Jr.) (goodreads.com).

[200] Duckworth, A., (2018). *Grit: The Power of Passion and Perseverance.* New York: Scribner.

Character combined with integrity and commitment sustains persistence and perseverance and ultimately makes it possible to achieve what others often fail to accomplish.

Character

+

Integrity

+

Commitment

Seven Qualities in Increasing Perseverance

Perseverance inspires and motivates others who observe its strength and its example encourages others to match its commitment. Megan Bruneau has identified seven qualities that lead to increased perseverance and that enhance the ability of a leader to sustain personal commitment[201].

1) The Ability to Find Meaning in the Process

Adversity confirms that a goal to be achieved has value and identifies the opportunity to discover that value. Seeking meaning in the process of perseverance facilitates overcoming the obstacles associated with accomplishing a worthy goal and makes it possible to achieve that goal more effectively in the future.

---

[201] Bruneau, M., (2016). "These 7 Qualities Lead to Perseverance when Faced with Adversity." *Forbes*, September 26, 2016 and found online on October 10, 2021 at These 7 Qualities Lead To Perseverance When Faced With Adversity (forbes.com).

Finding meaning in the process of perseverance facilitates overcoming the obstacles associated with accomplishing a worthy goal and makes it possible to achieve that goal more effectively in the future.

2) The Capacity to be Vulnerable, Connect with Others, and Ask for Help

Dealing with a difficult situation presents the opportunity to engage with others, to partner with them, to appreciate their capabilities, and to obtain their assistance. Being willing to ask for help and obtaining the cooperation of others can also teach the lesson that perseverance can be increased when working in partnership with others.

Being willing to ask for help and obtaining the cooperation of others can also teach the lesson that perseverance can be increased when working in partnership with others.

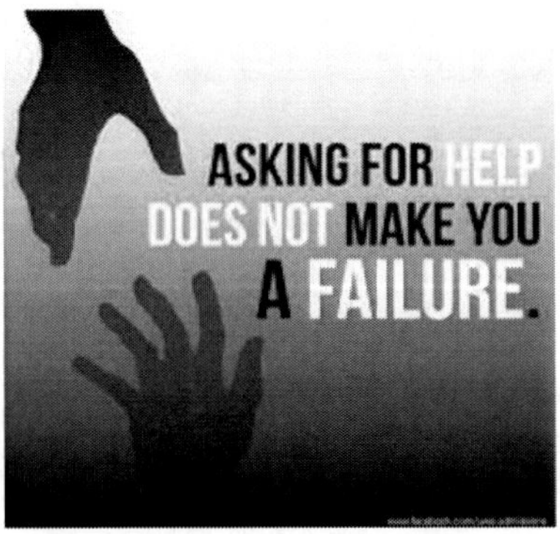

3) The Power to Create a Supportive Perception of Oneself

Treating oneself compassionately and avoiding beating oneself up when faced with a difficult challenge can strengthen the ability to endure, to assess opportunities to redirect efforts, and can reduce the stress associated with facing difficulties. The ability to look objectively at the efforts that one is making to "hang in there" can increase self-efficacy and self-esteem.

Treating oneself compassionately and **avoiding beating oneself up** when faced with a difficult challenge **can strengthen the ability to endure**, to **assess opportunities to redirect efforts,** and can **reduce the stress** associated with **facing difficulties**.

4) The Ability to Surrender and Trust in the Face of Difficulties

Acknowledging that there is much in life that is beyond one's ability to control is not only a reality of the world in which we live but is actually the opportunity to relieve stress and accept that truth. Assuming that the world is something within our ability to control creates immense pressure and responsibility – and simply is not true. We must be willing to surrender and trust.

Acknowledging that **there is much in life that is beyond one's ability to control** is not only a **reality of the world** in which we live but is actually **the opportunity to relieve stress** and **accept that truth.**

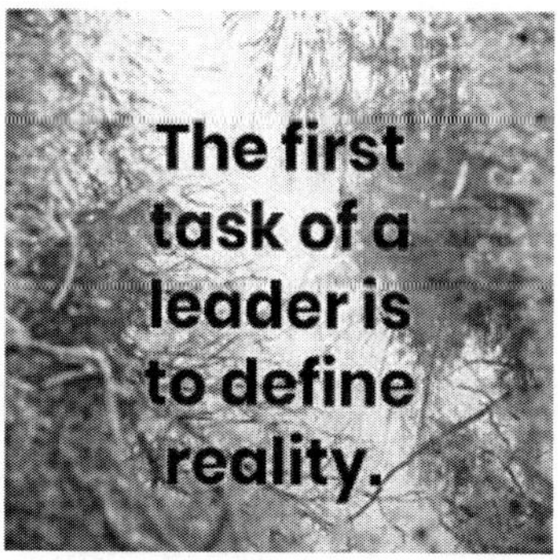

5) The Capacity to Develop a Sense of Humor about One's World

A sense of humor and the ability to laugh at oneself can not only relieve stress but can increase the capacity to be resilient. Humor can be used to create greater connection with others who can help to strengthen one's perseverance and can be the means of sharing pain and frustration in constructive ways.

Humor can be used to **create greater connection with others** who can help **to strengthen one's perseverance** and can be **the means of sharing pain and frustration** in **constructive ways.**

6) The Ability to Develop Mental Composure Despite Trials

The experience of struggling with achieving a goal and persisting in one's efforts can develop evenness of temper, mental calmness, and the ability to control one's mental and emotional perspective during difficult times. Increasing one's mindfulness, or the ability to be fully present and aware of what one is doing, enhances the capacity to persevere.

Struggling with achieving a goal and persisting in one's efforts **can develop evenness of temper, mental calmness**, and the **ability to control one's mental and emotional perspective** during **difficult times**.

7) The Capacity to Maintain Perspective and be Grateful

Difficult challenges and life's struggles provide context for the world and enable a person to see more clearly, despite adversity and trials. Adversity also makes it possible for a person to recognize the positive things that are present in life and to be grateful for that which one is able to accomplish or enjoy.

Adversity also **makes it possible** for a person to **recognize the positive** things that are present in life and to **be grateful** for **that which one is able to accomplish or enjoy.**

When properly understood, these seven qualities that accompany life's challenges can strengthen a person's capacity to endure and even to take necessary risks associated with the requirements of perseverance[202]. Acknowledging and fully embracing each of these seven qualities can make it possible for perseverance to be achievable until success finally comes and a goal is achieved.

Life's challenges can **strengthen a person's capacity to endure** and even to **take necessary risks** associated with **the requirements of perseverance.**

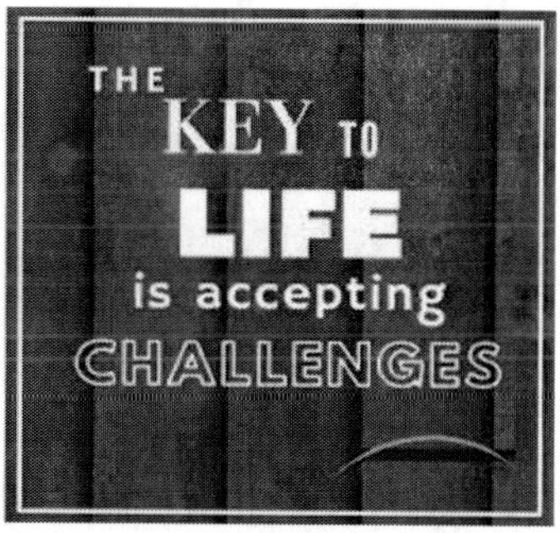

The Challenge to Persevere

Life's message is based upon the willingness to put into action the standards which ought to govern one's lives. The question, "How Will You Measure Your Life?" is ultimately answered by the choices that are made to endure, to

---

[202] *Ibid.*

persevere, and to be true to what we believe. Failure is the choice that occurs when we lack the willingness to honor what we say we believe.

Failure is the choice that occurs when we lack the willingness to honor what we say we believe.

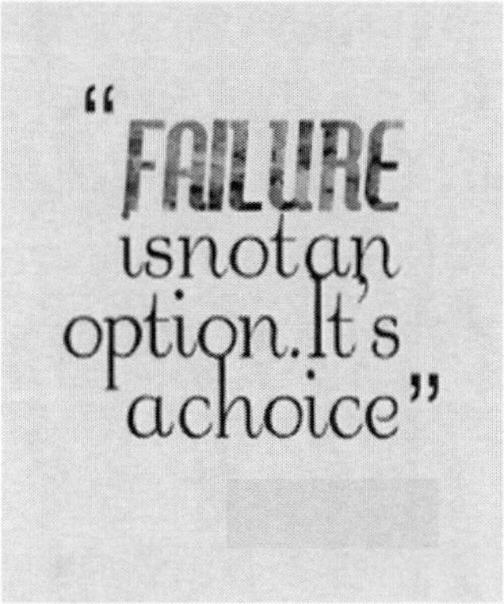

We challenge those who wish to earn the followership and respect of others to thoughtfully define what their lives truly mean. We challenge such leaders to develop the character, integrity, and commitment to be worthy of the mantle of leadership – demonstrated by honoring the values that they deem to be most sacred and that define their identity.

Understanding the qualities that make perseverance possible and **developing the character, commitment, and willingness** to achieve **one's highest potential** is **the gift** that great **leaders give to those whom they serve** – and that **they also give to themselves**.

Persistent and persevering are not easy. The ability to persevere with integrity is an acquired skill that is the result of clear thinking and personal effort. Understanding the qualities that make perseverance possible and developing the character, commitment, and willingness to achieve one's highest potential is the gift that great leaders give to those whom they serve – and that they also give to themselves.

References

Bandura, A. (1977). "Self-Efficacy: Toward a Unifying Theory of Behavioral Change." *Psychological Review*, Vol. 84, pp. 191-215.

Bruneau, M., (2016). "These 7 Qualities Lead to Perseverance when Faced with Adversity." *Forbes*, September 26, 2016 and found online on October 10, 2021 at These 7 Qualities Lead To Perseverance When Faced With Adversity (forbes.com).

Burke, P. J. & Stets, J. E., (2009). *Identity Theory*. Oxford, UK: Oxford University Press.

Carver, C. S. (1979). "A Cybernetic Model of Self-Attention Processes." *Journal of Personality and Social Psychology*, Vol. 37, pp. 1251-1281.

Christensen, C. M., Allworth, J. & Dillon, K., (2012). *How Will You Measure Your Life?* New York: Harper Business.

Duckworth, A., (2018). *Grit: The Power of Passion and Perseverance*. New York: Scribner.

Duckworth, A. L., Peterson, C., Matthews, M. D., & Kelly, D. R. (2007). "Grit: Perseverance and Passion for Long-term Goals." *Journal of Personality and Social Psychology*, Vol. 92, pp. 1087- 1101.

Fishbein, M. & Ajzen, I., (2015). *Predicting and Changing Behavior: The Reasoned Action Approach*. New York: Psychology Press.

King, M. & Carruthers, P., (2012). "Moral Responsibility and Consciousness." *Journal of Moral Philosophy*, Vol. 9, pp. 200-228.

Kleckner, J., (2018). "80 Albert Einstein Quotes to Inspire You for Life." Addicted2Success, December 18, 2018 and found online on October 10, 2021 at 80 Albert Einstein Quotes to Inspire You For Life (addicted2success.com),

Kupperman, J., (1995). *Character*. Oxford, UK: Oxford University Press.

Lufi, D. & Cohen, A., (1987). "A Scale for Measuring Persistence in Children." *Journal of Personality Assessment*, Vol. 51, No. 2, pp. 178-185.

Meier, G. & Albrecht. M. H., (2003). "The Persistence Process: Development of a Stage Model for Goal-Directed Behavior." *Journal of Leadership and Organizational Studies*, Vol. 10, No. 2, pp. 43-54.

Stone, B. & Ukleja, M., (2009). *The Ethics Challenge: Strengthening Your Integrity in a Greedy World*. New York: Morgan James Publishing.

Sylvester, B., (2019). "Fact Check: Did Aristotle Say 'We are what we repeatedly do?'" CheckYourFact, June 16, 2019 and found online on October 10, 2021 at FACT CHECK: Did Aristotle Say, 'We Are What We Repeatedly Do'? | Check Your Fact.

Vroom, V. (1964). *Work and Motivation*. New York, NY: Wiley and Sons.

Chapter 6

Serving with Passion

The greatest leaders are servants first[203]. This adage about the the leader as the servant of others has captured the attention of modern leadership scholars for decades and has its roots in the philosophy of leaders for millennia[204]. Servant leadership is known for its commitment to the welfare of individuals in organizations, as well as the achievement of an organization's mission and purpose. Those who adopt this leadership perspective embrace its highly moral perspective about duties owed to others and view the commitment associated with leadership as a "covenantal responsibility[205]."

The greatest leaders are servants first. This adage about the importance of the leader as the servant of others has captured the attention of modern leadership scholars for decades and has its roots in the philosophy of leaders for millennia.

We begin the chapter by describing the nature of servant leadership and explaining seven fundamental pillars upon which servant leadership is based. We then identify eight important ways that the servant leader perspective establishes better relationships and builds more effective organizations. The chapter concludes with a challenge to leaders to incorporate servant leadership in honoring their responsibilities to their organizations and to those with whom they work.

---

[203] Greenleaf, R. K., (2002). *Servant Leadership: A Journey into the Nature of Legitimate Power and Greatness 25th Anniversary Edition*. Mahwah, NJ: Paulist Press.
[204] *Ibid.*
[205] DePree, M., (2004). *Leadership is an Art*. New York: Crown Publishing.

Understanding Servant Leadership

Although servant leadership is a relatively new leadership theory, the importance of serving others has been a major priority of effective leadership for millennia[206]. Robert Greenleaf explained that the "great leader was servant first, because that was what he was *deep down inside*[207]." (Italics in the original.)

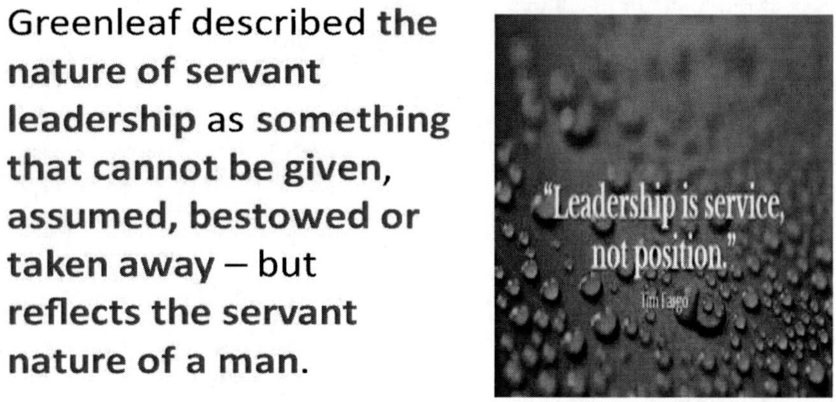

Greenleaf described the nature of servant leadership as something that cannot be given, assumed, bestowed or taken away – but reflects the servant nature of a man[208]. Greenleaf clarified how the commitment to servant leadership evolves within a person.

> It begins with the natural feeling that one wants to serve, to serve first. Then conscious choice brings one to aspire to lead. That person is sharply different from one who is leader first, perhaps because of the need to assuage an unusual power drive or to acquire material possessions . . . The Leader First and the Servant First are two extreme types. Between them there are shadings and blends that are part of the infinite variety of human nature[209].

---

[206] Frick, Don M. (2004). *Robert K. Greenleaf: A Life of Servant Leadership.* San Francisco: Berrett-Koehler Publishers.

[207] *Ibid.* p. 7.

[208] Greenleaf, R. K., (2015). *The Servant as Leader.* Indianapolis, IN: The Greenleaf Center for Servant Leadership, p. 2.

[209] *Ibid.*

In his efforts to clarify why leaders who serve are so effective, Greenleaf explained that servant leaders strive to help others to become healthier, wiser, and more likely to become leaders themselves[210]. Greenleaf wrote that "only a true natural servant automatically responds to a problem by listening first[211]." Servant leaders willingly listen to others' ideas and seek to understand them. In relating to others, servant leaders also show great compassion. Although they may not always be satisfied with others' actions, they nonetheless accept and care about others as individuals[212].

In understanding service and leadership, it is helpful to think of service to others as a derivative of the leader's perspective about life's purpose.

In understanding service and leadership, it is helpful to think of service to others as a derivative of the leader's perspective about life's purpose[213]. Marcus Aurelius explained that service to others has its roots in the divinity that lies within each individual[214]. It is in serving that a person believes that (s)he is fulfilling that divine purpose and that one's life ought to be spent in making a better world[215]. Service, then, becomes an effort to fulfill the common good and reflects the acknowledgement of the unity of man and the harmony that is found in all facets of life[216].

---

210 Greenleaf, R.K., (2007). "The Servant as Leader." In W. C. Zimmerli, K. Richter & M. Holzinger, (Eds.) *Corporate Ethics and Corporate Governance*. New York: Springer, pp. 79–85

211 Greenleaf, R. K., (2015), *op. cit.,* p. 8.

212 *Ibid.* p. 12.

213 Aurelius, M., (2019). *Meditations.* New York: SDE Classics.

214 *Ibid.*

215 *Ibid.*

216 *Ibid.*

Servant Leadership's Seven Pillars

The value of any leadership perspective lies in its application – which affirms the leader's practical value. Leaders are effective when they connect with others on a personal level and establish a reputation for being worthy of others' trust[217]. The means by which servant leadership is able to connect with individuals is by putting their needs first. As servant leaders demonstrate that they are competent, caring, and committed to others' best interests they strengthen that connection[218].

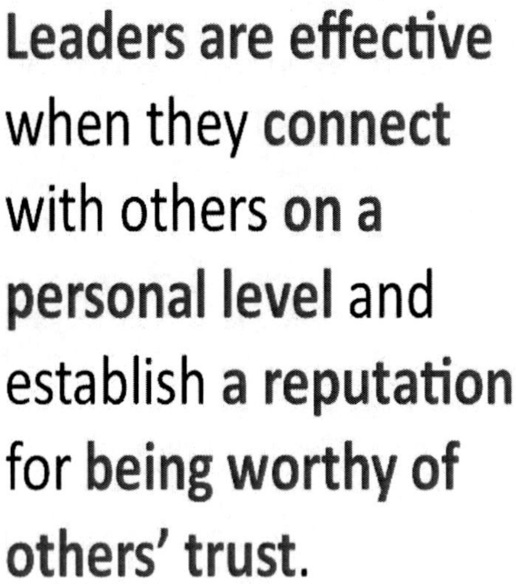

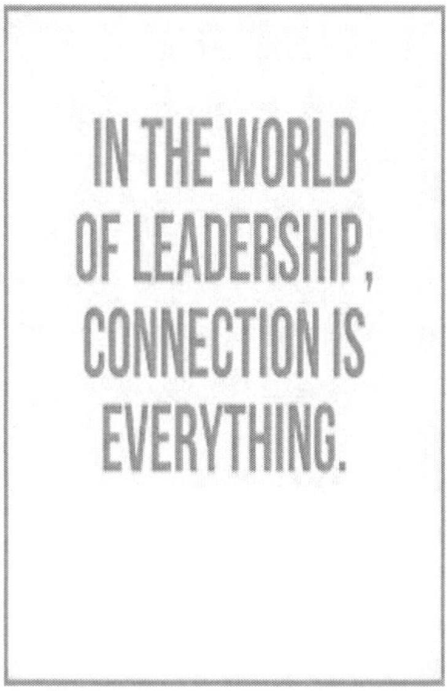

In their book about servant leadership, James Sipe and Don Frick have identified seven pillars upon which servant leadership is founded[219].

[217] MBayer, R. C., Davis, J. H. & Schoorman, F. D., (1995). "An Integrative Model of Organizational Trust." *Academy of Management Review*, Vol. 20, No. 3, pp. 709-734.
[218] Caldwell, C., and Ndalamba, K. K., (2017). "Trust and Being 'Worthy' – The Keys to Creating Wealth." *Journal of Management Development*, Vol. 36, Iss. 8, pp. 1076-1086.
[219] Sipe, J. W. & Frick, D. M., (2015). *Seven Pillars of Servant Leadership: Practicing the Wisdom of Leading by Serving; Revised and Expanded Edition*. Mahwah, NJ: Paulist Press.

1) Character

The importance of character includes integrity in honoring commitments, modeling the values that are proclaimed, and telling the truth. In serving others, the servant leader demonstrates personal character by consistently demonstrating a commitment to doing what's right and speaking the truth. The servant leader honors obligations owed to people, rather than simply focusing on the organization's results.

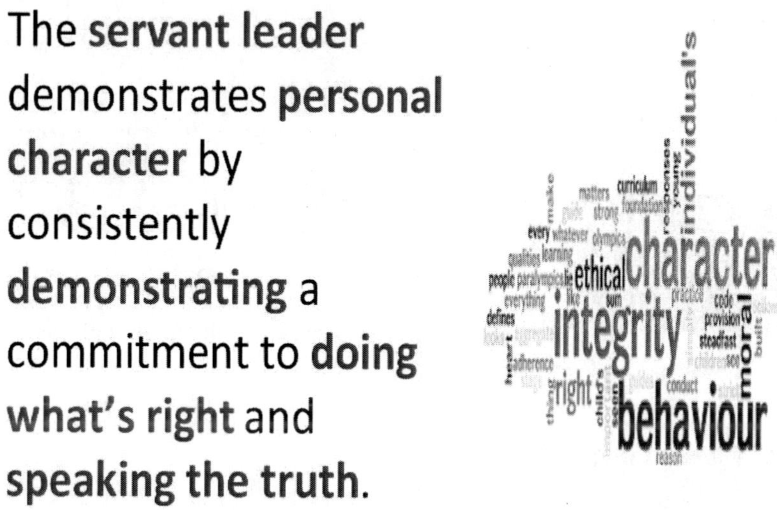

2) Selflessness

Selflessness is constantly exemplified by servant leaders as they put others' needs above their own and seek to help others to be more fulfilled, more successful, and more capable members of their organization. Rather than focusing on their own reputation and looking good in the eyes of others, servant leaders help others to become their best selves and look for opportunities to contribute to their growth. By putting others first, the servant leader demonstrates a caring commitment to others' needs and acknowledges the importance of others' roles in contributing to the success of an organization.

By **putting others first**, the servant leader **demonstrates a caring commitment** to others' needs and **acknowledges the importance of others' roles** in **contributing to the success of an organization**.

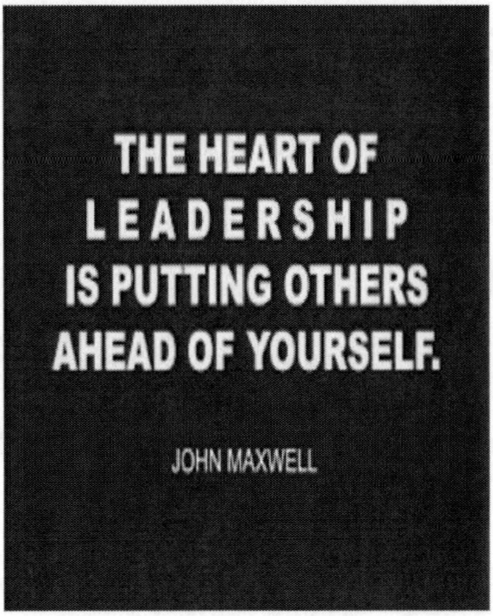

3) Communication

Servant leaders strive to identify the needs of others, actively seek out their opinions, and listen carefully to their thoughts. Communication is two-way, but servant leaders recognize that their ability to create powerful relationships begins by being available and by communicating their commitment to others by their actions as well as by their words. By listening as well as (s)he communicates, the servant leader understands the needs of others and is persuasive and effective.

Servant leaders **recognize that their ability to create** powerful **relationships** begins by **being available** and by **communicating their commitment to others by their actions as well as by their words.**

4) Compassion

Compassion includes the ability to not only understand others' needs and to be able to put themselves in others' position, but includes identifying the most effective way to respond to their needs and concerns. Compassion enables servant leaders to go the extra mile in helping those whom they serve when the leader's assistance is needed. Compassion demonstrates care by doing much more than conveying concern. Effective compassion creates a sense of mutual commitment among members, enhances community, and creates a sense of belonging.

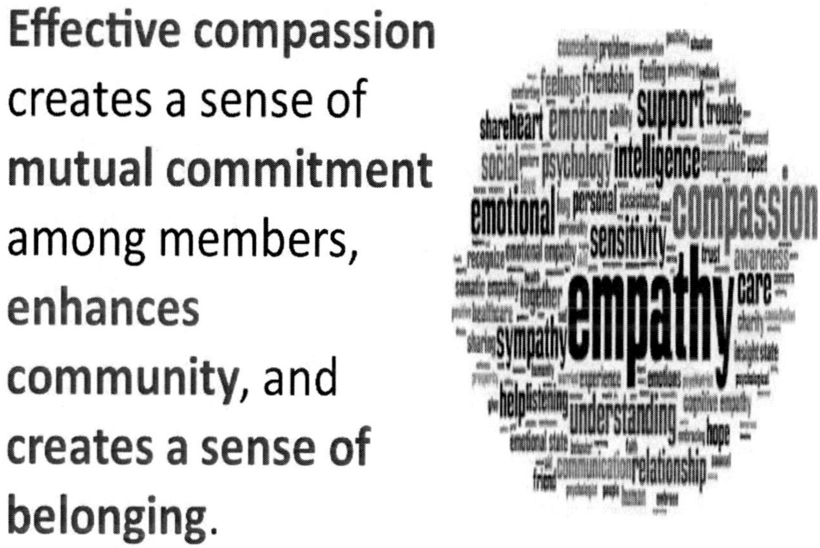

5) Foresight

Foresight is the ability to link the past and the present together and to use that insight to accurately anticipate the future. By paying attention to patterns and by being intuitive in their awareness of situations and context, servant leaders are able to use wisdom in identifying future outcomes and preparing for those outcomes so that others' needs are met. The foresight of a servant leader enables the leader to demonstrate both creativity and courage in anticipating future priorities.

By paying attention to patterns and by being intuitive in their awareness of situations and context, servant leaders are able to use wisdom in identifying future outcomes and preparing for those outcomes so that others' needs are met.

6) Systems-Focused

The ability to look at the interrelationship of events and the context of situations is a part of the servant leader's systems focus. Servant leaders recognize that organization systems need to match the values upon which an organization is based if that organization and the leader are to be perceived as credible. Aligning systems conveys the servant leader's commitment to others while working to achieve the greatest good for the organization. The servant leader is comfortable with complexity and able to adapt, as needed.

The ability to look at the interrelationship of events and the context of situations is a part of the servant leader's systems focus.

7) Moral Authority

Moral authority of servant leaders is demonstrated by their commitment to being stewards that care for the long-term needs of their organization, the sustainability of its purpose, and the importance of individuals who contribute to the organization's success. The servant leader's moral authority is derived from commitment to the community, honoring true principles, and exemplifying the standards that (s)he expects of others. Accountability is a priority of moral authority and organization members willingly accept responsibility as they adopt the leader's example.

Accountability is a **priority of moral authority** and organization **members** willingly **accept responsibility** as they **adopt the leader's example.**

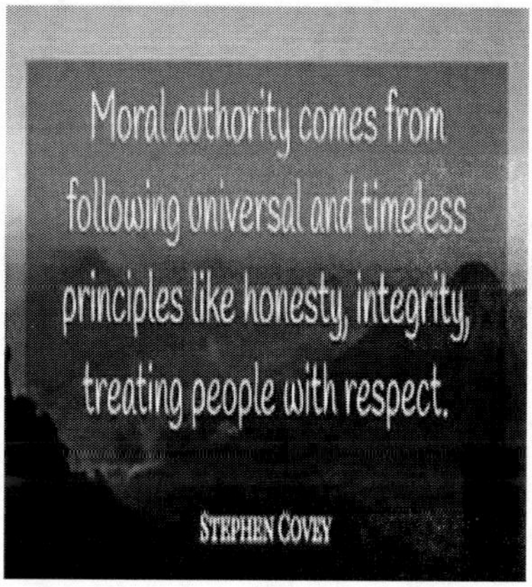

Each of these seven pillars contributes to the servant leader's ability to demonstrate that (s)he is committed to the organization and to each of its members. The seven pillars contribute to the servant leader's ability to integrate organizational strategy and culture[220].

Servant Leadership Matters

Servant leaders view their role as both a privilege and a responsibility[221]. By their example, their personal integrity, and their commitment to service, they demonstrate the ideals that not only create organizations that create value but that inspire others to follow in their footsteps.

---

220 *Ibid.*

221 Greenleaf, R. K., (1996). "The Requirements of Responsibility." In D. M. Frick & L. C. Spears (Eds.), *On Becoming a Servant Leader*. San Francisco, CA: Jossey-Bass, pp. 41-52.

The following are eight ways in which the servant leader perspective contributes to individuals and organizations.

1) It Affirms the Worth and Potential of Others

By putting service over their own personal self-interest, servant leaders demonstrate that they value others' worth and recognize their almost unlimited potential[222]. As servant leaders treat others as valued partners, they convey to their colleagues the message that they are respected, honored, and appreciated[223]. In the words of J. Carla Northcutt, "The role of a great leader is to help people to think more highly of themselves[224]."

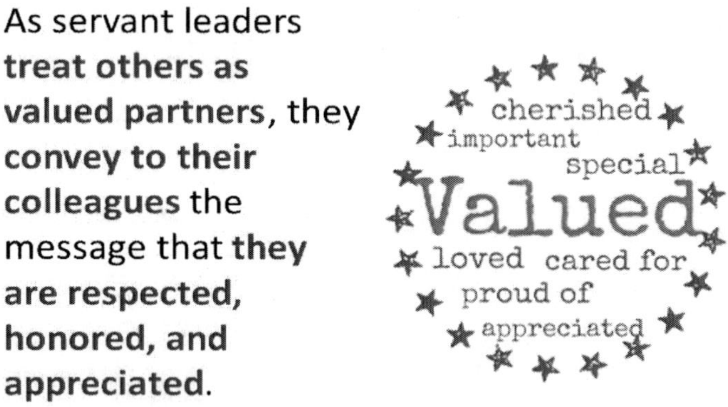

[222] Block, P., (2013). *Stewardship: Choosing Service Over Self-Interest*. San Francisco, CA: Jossey-Bass.

[223] *Ibid.*

[224] J. Carla Northcutt. Pinterest.com. Found online on October 13, 2021 at "The goal of many leaders is to get people to think more highly of the leader. The goal of a great leader is to h... | Helping people, Leadership coaching, Leadership (pinterest.com),

2) It emphasizes the importance of shared interests.

Servant leaders' willingness to listen to others and to incorporate their insights into improving an organization demonstrates that they view the relationship with employees as a shared interest and mutual responsibility[225]. Although servant leaders care greatly about the organization, they also understand that the most effective way to achieve its goals is by creating partnerships with employees rather than treating them as subordinates and underlings[226].

Servant leaders' **willingness to listen** to others and **to incorporate their insights** into improving an organization **demonstrates that they view the relationship** with employees as **a shared interest and mutual responsibility.**

3) It Engages Others as Empowered Participants

Servant leaders recognize the importance of engaging and empowering employees by giving them responsibilities and by preparing them to be accountable for results[227]. Such leaders understand that fully involved and empowered employees are critical if an organization is going to be able to fulfill its potential[228]. As John Maxwell has explained, "Leaders do not become great because of their power but because of their ability to empower others[229]."

225 Greenleaf, R. K., (2015), *op. cit.*, p. 8.

226 Block, P., (2013), *op. cit.*

227 Greenleaf, R. K., (1996), *op. cit.*

228 Clifton, J. & Harter, J., (2019). *It's the Manager*. Omaha, NE: Gallup Press.

229 "John C. Maxwell Quotes." *Goodreads.com*. Found online on October 13, 2021 at Quote by John Maxwell: "A leader is great not because of his or her pow..." (goodreads.com),

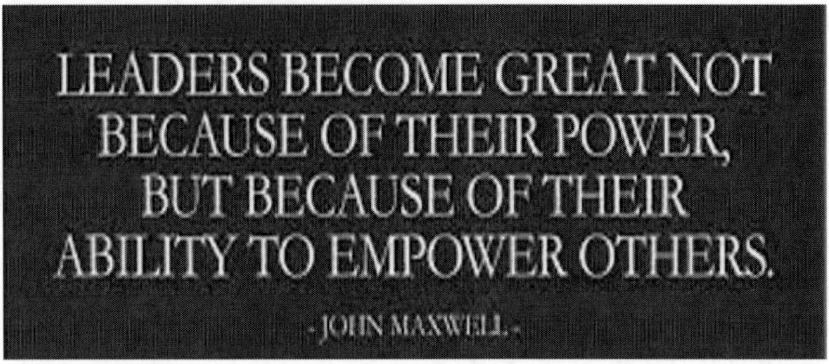

4) It Seeks Others' Welfare, Growth, and Wholeness

In writing about the obligation that servant leaders owe to their colleagues, Max DePree explained that organizational leaders had a "covenantal duty" to work for their employees' best interests[230]. Demonstrating their commitment to the welfare, growth, and wholeness of others is the means by which leaders honor their employees and convey that those leaders authentically love and care about employees and their priorities[231]. This ability to genuinely love others sustains leaders and their role in organizations[232].

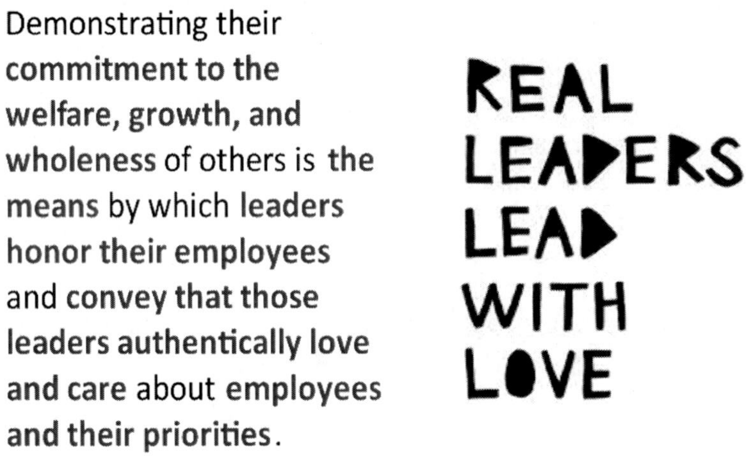

[230] DePree, M., (2004), *op. cit.*

[231] Caldwell, C. & Anderson, V., (2019). "Love: The Heart of Leadership – Introduction and Overview" in C. Caldwell & V. Anderson (Eds.), *Leading with Love*. Hauppauge, NY: NOVA Publishers, Chapter 1.

[232] James Kouzes. "20 Servant Leadership Quotes that Elevate Our Thinking." *RickConlow.com.* Found online on October 13, 2021 at 20 Servant Leadership Quotes that Elevate our Thinking - Rick Conlow. *Ibid.*

5) It Honors the Organization's Mission and Purpose.

Servant leadership emphasizes the purpose and mission of an organization. The leader exemplifies that commitment by her/his personal dedication to that mission[233]. By that personal commitment, the servant leader conveys to colleagues her/his dedication, passion, and ownership of the goals of the organization and inspires others to do likewise. Clarity of purpose gives meaning, perspective, and a sense of belonging to others.

Servant leadership emphasizes the purpose and mission of an organization and the servant leader **exemplifies that commitment** by her/his **personal dedication** to that mission.

6) It Communicates by Action and Example

The ability of leaders to model the way is a critical element of successful leadership and communicates the legitimacy of the leader's character[234]. Communicating by example is far more effective than simply issuing directives[235]. The servant leader's willingness to listen and to apply what (s)he is hearing inspires others' trust as well[236]. In the words of Marian Anderson, "Leadership should be born out of the understanding of the needs of those who would be affected by it[237]."

---

[233] Greenleaf, R. K., (2015), *op. cit.*

[234] Kouzes, J. M. & Posner, B. Z., (2017). *The Leadership Challenge: How to Make Extraordinary Things Happen in Organizations* (7th ed.). San Francisco, CA: Jossey-Bass, pp. 45-92.

[235] *Ibid.*

[236] Greenleaf, R. K., (2015), *op. cit.*

[237] Marian Anderson. "20 Servant Leadership Quotes that Elevate Our Thinking." *RickConlow.com.* Found online on October 13, 2021 at 20 Servant Leadership Quotes that Elevate our Thinking - Rick Conlow.

The ability of a leader to model the way is a critical element of successful leadership and communicates the legitimacy of the leader's character.

7) It Exemplifies Virtuousness and Moral Conduct

An authentic servant leader is dedicated to those people whom the leader willingly serves and the leader's strength of character communicates her/his moral identity[238]. Servant leaders believe that they owe a quasi-sacred set of obligations to others[239]. They readily acknowledge that the strength of their personal example and their commitment to moral conduct is critical to their credibility as leaders[240]. Great leaders inspire others to learn more, dream more, and do more[241].

Great leaders inspire others to learn more, dream more, and do more.

---

238 *Ibid.*

239 Greenleaf, R. K., (2002), *op. cit.*

240 DePree, M., (2004), *op. cit.*

241 John Quincy Adams Quotes (Leadership). GraciousQuotes,com. Found online on October 13, 2021 at 30 John Quincy Adams Quotes (LEADERSHIP) (graciousquotes.com).

8) It Aligns with True Principles and Inspiring Values

True principles and values have the ability to inspire and motivate others to raise their own standards of personal conduct[242]. The actions of authentic servant leaders ring true with those with whom they work and align with what their colleagues recognize as honorable standards of conduct. For that reason, others admire, respect, and trust true servant leaders[243]. It is by focusing on principles that leaders empower others[244].

The actions of authentic servant leaders ring true with those with whom they work and align with what their colleagues recognize as honorable standards of conduct.

Leaders who consistently practice servant leadership and who demonstrate a commitment to the welfare of those with whom they work are more often than not viewed as highly unique in today's world where so many employees distrust their leaders, managers, and supervisors[245]. By incorporating the principles of servant leadership, those who adopt its tenets find that those tenets enable them to benefit their organizations and increase employee commitment in these eight important ways.

---

[242] Covey, S. R., (2004). *The 8th Habit: From Effectiveness to Greatness*. New York: Free Press.
[243] Block, P., (2013), *op. cit.*
[244] "Stephen Covey Principles Quotes." LibQuotes.com. Found online on October 13, 2021 at Stephen Covey Quotes about Principles - Lib Quotes.
[245] Clifton, J. & Harter, J., (2019), *op. cit.*

By incorporating the principles of servant leadership, those who adopt its tenets find that they enable them to benefit their organizations and increase employee commitment.

The Servant Leadership Challenge

The passion to lead is most effective when it is focused on accomplishing a worthy outcome that enriches the lives of others and makes an important contribution in the world. To be a great leader, one assists others to grow and to share in the achievements that benefit the world around them. The Chinese philosopher, Lao Tzu, suggested that "A leader is best when people barely know he exists, when his work is done, his aim fulfilled, they will say: 'We did it ourselves.'" Servant leaders, like the one that Lao Tzu describes, empower those with whom they work and care more about what is accomplished than who gets the credit.

The passion to lead is most effective when it is focused on accomplishing a worthy outcome that enriches the lives of others and makes an important contribution in the world. To be a great leader, one assists others to grow and to share in the achievements that benefit the world around them.

We challenge those who wish to lead to contemplate their own assumptions about leadership and service. We invite those individuals to carefully study the seven pillars of servant leadership and to identify the degree to which they incorporate the insights contained in those pillars in their own leadership approach. We suggest that the eight ways that servant leaders make a difference in the lives of individuals and organizations are simple truths that can help those who seek to lead to be far more effective. Servant leadership succeeds as a leadership perspective because it values people and empowers them to be full partners in the process of making a valuable contribution to their colleagues, to their organizations, and to the world.

Servant leadership succeeds as a leadership perspective **because it values people** and **empowers them to be full partners** in the process of making **a valuable contribution to their colleagues**, to **their organizations**, and to **the world**.

References

"Stephen Covey Principles Quotes." LibQuotes.com. Found online on October 13, 2021 at Stephen Covey Quotes about Principles - Lib Quotes.

Anderson, Marian. "20 Servant Leadership Quotes that Elevate Our Thinking." *RickConlow.com.* Found online on October 13, 2021 at 20 Servant Leadership Quotes that Elevate our Thinking - Rick Conlow.

Aurelius, M., (2019). *Meditations*. New York: SDE Classics.

Bayer, R. C., Davis, J. H. & Schoorman, F. D., (1995). "An Integrative Model of Organizational Trust." *Academy of Management Review*, Vol. 20, No. 3, pp. 709-734.

Block, P., (2013). *Stewardship: Choosing Service Over Self-Interest.* San Francisco, CA: Jossey-Bass.

Caldwell, C. & Anderson, V., (2019). "Love: The Heart of Leadership – Introduction and Overview" in C. Caldwell & V. Anderson (Eds.), *Leading with Love*. Hauppauge, NY: NOVA Publishers, Chapter 1.

Caldwell, C., and Ndalamba, K. K., (2017). "Trust and Being 'Worthy' – The Keys to Creating Wealth." *Journal of Management Development*, Vol. 36, Iss. 8, pp. 1076-1086.

Clifton, J. & Harter, J., (2019). *It's the Manager*. Omaha, NE: Gallup Press.

Covey, S. R., (2004). *The 8th Habit: From Effectiveness to Greatness*. New York: Free Press.

DePree, M., (2004). *Leadership is an Art*. New York: Crown Publishing.

Frick, Don M. (2004). *Robert K. Greenleaf: A Life of Servant Leadership*. San Francisco: Berrett-Koehler Publishers.

Greenleaf, R. K., (1996). "The Requirements of Responsibility." In D. M. Frick & L. C. Spears (Eds.), *On Becoming a Servant Leader*. San Francisco, CA: Jossey-Bass, pp. 41-52.

Greenleaf, R. K., (2002). *Servant Leadership: A Journey into the Nature of Legitimate Power and Greatness 25th Anniversary Edition*. Mahwah, NJ: Paulist Press.

Greenleaf, R.K., (2007). "The Servant as Leader." In W. C. Zimmerli, K. Richter & M. Holzinger, (Eds.) *Corporate Ethics and Corporate Governance*. New York: Springer, pp. 79–85.

James Kouzes. "20 Servant Leadership Quotes that Elevate Our Thinking." *RickConlow.com.* Found online on October 13, 2021 at 20 Servant Leadership Quotes that Elevate our Thinking - Rick Conlow.

John Quincy Adams Quotes (Leadership). GraciousQuotes,com. Found online on October 13, 2021 at 30 John Quincy Adams Quotes (LEADERSHIP) (graciousquotes.com).

Kouzes, J. M. & Posner, B. Z., (2017). *The Leadership Challenge: How to Make Extraordinary Things Happen in Organizations* (7th ed.). San Francisco, CA: Jossey-Bass, pp. 45-92.

Sipe, J. W. & Frick, D. M., (2015). *Seven Pillars of Servant Leadership: Practicing the Wisdom of Leading by Serving; Revised and Expanded Edition*. Mahwah, NJ: Paulist Press.

Chapter 7

Hope as a Form of Passion

Hope, though frequently not fully understood, is a motivating force that drives action – even when evidence may be lacking about the subject of that hope. People hope for that which they yearn for and for that which they deem possible. Aristotle called hope "a waking dream" in which men and women create a future that may be unlikely to come[246]. Hope, according to Aristotle, was an amalgam that involved optimism, courage, and fear[247].

Hope, though frequently **not fully understood**, is a **motivating force that drives action** – even when **evidence may be lacking** about the subject of that hope.

The purpose of this chapter is to provide insights about the nature of hope as a resource to leaders. Although hope may be an elusive concept, it nonetheless has been the motivation for human effort and positive expectations for millennia. We begin the chapter by defining hope as it applies in individual lives. We identify seven attributes of hope that refine its definition in the practical world. We then suggest five positive qualities of hope that are assets to leadership but also identify how relying on hope can be

[246] "Aristotle Quotes." Goodreads.com. Found online on October 14, 2021 at Aristotle Quotes (Author of The Nicomachean Ethics) (goodreads.com).

[247] Bock, C., (2016). "Hope in Ancient Greece: Aristotle on Hope, Optimism, and Courage." April 25, 2016 and found online on October 14, 2021 at Hope in Ancient Greek: Aristotle on hope, optimism, and courage – Cherice Bock.

dysfunctional for leaders and organizations when hope is not viewed realistically. The chapter concludes by encouraging leaders to understand the nature and limits of hope.

Understanding Hope

Hope is the desire to attain a future outcome accompanied by the expectation that the outcome will come to pass[248]. In acknowledging the difficulty of maintaining hope under trying circumstances, South Africa's Desmond Tutu called hope the ability to see the light in the presence of darkness[249]. Hope's capacity to look to the positive, despite e an uncertain future, that enables hope to be a source of comfort and motivation.

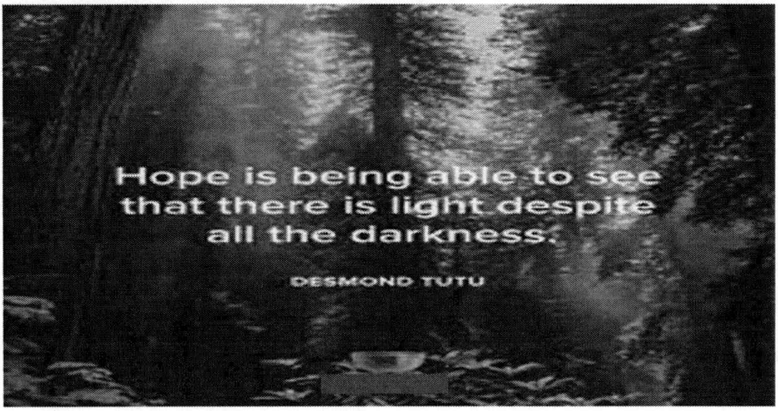

Hope is a compound attitude composed of rationally conceived and intentionally soughtafter elements[250]. Hope is more than the expectation that a desired outcome will occur but includes the desire to achieve that outcome[251]. Hope cushions the heart and mind in times when evidence of the

---

[248] "Hope." YourDictionary.com. Found online on October 14, 2021 at Hope Meaning | Best 35 Definitions of Hope (yourdictionary.com).

[249] "Desmond Tutu Quotes." *BrainyQuotes.com*. Found online on October 14, 2021 at Desmond Tutu Quotes - BrainyQuote.

[250] Bloeser, C. & Stahl, T., (2017). "Hope." In E. N. Zalta, (Ed.). The Stanford Encyclopedia of Philosophy. Found online on October 14, 2021 at Author and Citation Information for "Hope" (stanford.edu).

[251] *Ibid.*

likelihood of a future outcome may not be present. Hope inspires and sustains, even when times may be painful and difficult[252].

Hope cushions the heart and mind in times when evidence of the likelihood of a future outcome may not be present. Hope inspires and sustains, even when times may be painful and difficult.

hope sustains life

Hope contains elements of optimism but is also substantially different. Bloeser and Stahl identify the distinction between the two terms[253].

> "While optimism can be usefully analyzed as a desire for an outcome together with a belief that the outcome is more likely than not (or more likely than the evidence leads other people to believe), many philosophers argue that hope, properly understood, is independent of probability assessments. One can hope for outcomes that one considers to be very unlikely and that one does not expect to happen, such as a miraculous cure of an illness. In such cases, optimism is not an appropriate response."

Thus, hope may not be entirely rational in its predictive logic but reflects the desires of the heart rather than the analysis of the mind[254].

---

[252] "Laini Taylor Quotes." *BrainyQuotes.com*. Found online on October 24, 2021 at TOP 25 QUOTES BY LAINI TAYLOR (of 242) | A-Z Quotes (azquotes.com).

[253] Bloeser, C. & Stahl, T., (2017), *op. cit.*

[254] *Ibid.*

Hope reflects wishful thinking and **may include perceptions** about **the nature of God** and the **divine principles upon which** a person believes that **the world is based.**

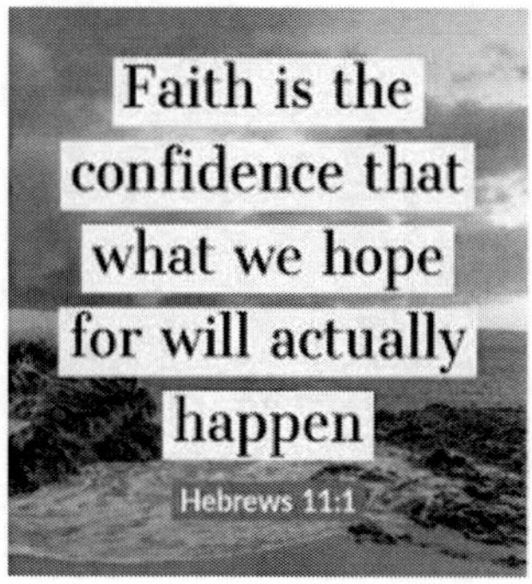

Hope reflects wishful thinking and may include perceptions about the nature of God and the divine principles upon which a person believes that the world is based[255]. Religious philosophers viewed hope as a central virtue of Christian believers and argued that its rationality is essential to the nature of faith. Sir Thomas Aquinas described hope as an "irascible passion" rather than a mere desire[256] and viewed hope as a habit of the will that is preceded by faith in God[257]. Hope, within the religious context, is the antithesis of fear, despair, and doubt and includes a future-directed belief that a better world is possible[258].

Philosophers of the 17th and 18th century viewed hope as a motivating passion reflecting emotions and desires rather than cognitive thought[259]. In Descartes' *Passions of the Soul*, he defined hope as the desire for an outcome that was both positive and possible – but was always accompanied by anxiety[260]. Hobbes referred to hope as associated with the pursuit of appetites or perceived physical needs[261]. Spinoza defined hope as a passion of pleasure or joy – but noted that it was often accompanied by sadness and fear about

---

[255] Caldwell, C., Davis, B., and Devine, J. A., (2009). "Trust, Faith, and Betrayal: Insights from Management for the Wise Believer." *Journal of Business Ethics*, Vol. 89, Iss. 1, pp. 103-114.

[256] Aquinas, T., (1956). *Scriptum super Sententiis.* Lethielleux-Rousteau, France: Lethielleux Publishers, SsS III, 26.

[257] Aquinas, T., (2012). *Summa Theologiae Prima Pars.* Dubuque, IA: Emmaus Academic, ST II-II 17.6.

[258] Bloeser, C. & Stahl, T., (2017), *op. cit.*

[259] *Ibid.*

[260] Descartes, R. & Moriarty, M., (2016) *The Passions of the Soul and Other Late Philosophical Writings*. Oxford, UK: Oxford University Press.

[261] Hobbes, T. & Schneider, H. W., (2017). *Leviathan*. Boston, MA: Digireads.com Publishing, Chapter LVI.14.

one's present state[262]. Hume described hope as combining both joy and sorrow – based upon the likelihood of whether a hoped-for outcome would occur[263].

Maintaining hope benefits individuals in the present time because it creates within them a positive view of themselves and the world that is far better than negative feelings of fear, uncertainty, and unhappiness.

William James viewed hope as much like faith[264] and described both faith and hope as consisting of: 1) the inability to determine a desired outcome scientifically, 2) the belief that what is believed or hoped for may nonetheless be true, and 3) the positive benefit, even if in the present, that would accrue if a person believes[265]. Maintaining hope, James suggested, benefits individuals in the present time because it creates within them a positive view of themselves and the world that is far better than negative feelings of fear, uncertainty, and unhappiness[266]. Though a hoped-for outcome may not occur, James argued that the sustaining hope improves an individual's quality of life.

Ariel Meirav described hope as a desire that a beneficial event would occur, coupled with the probability of that event[267]. Summarizing the "standard argument" about hope, Meirav suggested that the distinction between hope and despair lies in each individual's perceptions about what is possible and the likelihood of an external factor influencing a desired

---

262 Spinoza, B. & Elwes, R. H. M., (2021). *Ethics*, Chapter III, p. 18.

263 Hume, David, [1738] (2007). *A Treatise of Human Nature*. In D.F. Norton and M.J. Norton (Eds.). Oxford. UK Oxford University Press,

264 James, W., (2015). *The Will to Believe and Other Essays in Popular Philosophy*: New York: Dover Publications.

265 *Ibid.*

266 *Ibid.*

267 Meirav, A., (2009). "The Nature of Hope." *Ratio: An International Journal of Analytic Philosophy*. Vol. 22, Iss. 2, pp. 216-233.

outcome[268]. He concluded that despair was the loss of hope. Luc Bovens observed that, while hope may not have instrumental value in contributing to the achievement of a desired outcome, it may have intrinsic value that benefits individuals because it 1) promotes positive and pleasurable mental imaging, 2) increases self-awareness and associated self-understanding, and 3) promotes positive feelings and love toward others and towards oneself[269].

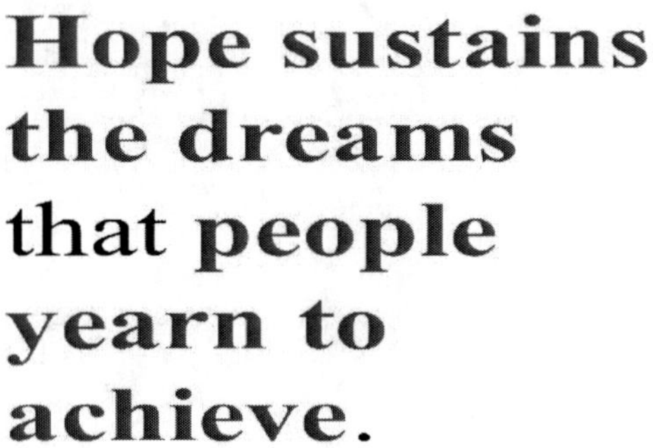

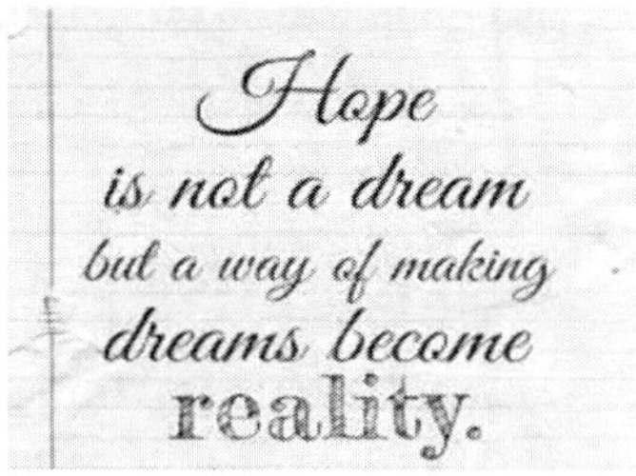

As a phenomenon that enables individuals to maintain positive expectations about an uncertain world, hope can become a source of comfort for individuals who seek outcomes that may be unlikely but that are passionately desired. Hope sustains dreams that people yearn to achieve. The importance of hope in the human story has been poignantly described by Boston University's Howard Zinn.

> "To be hopeful in bad times is not just foolishly romantic. It is based on the fact that human history is a history not only of cruelty, but also of compassion, sacrifice, courage, kindness. What we choose to emphasize in this complex history will determine our lives. If we see only the worst, it destroys our capacity to do something. If we remember those times and places—and there are so many—where people have behaved magnificently, this gives us the energy to act, and at least the possibility of sending this spinning top of a world in a different direction. And if we do act, in however small a way, we don't have to wait for some grand utopian future. The future is an infinite succession of presents, and to live now as we think human beings should live, in defiance of all that is bad around us, is itself a marvelous victory."

---

[268] Ibid.
[269] *Ibid.*

Hope enables men and women to look for the good, despite the world's shortcomings, disappointments, and pain. Though that which is hoped for may not always come to pass, hope can inspire, motivate, and enable individuals to endure life's trials with grace and courage – and by doing so can enable those individuals to achieve a personal victory even when what one hopes for is not realized.

Though that which is hoped for **may not always come to pass**, hope can **inspire, motivate, and enable** individuals to **endure life's trials with grace and courage** -- and by so doing can **enable those individuals to achieve a personal victory** even when **what one hopes for is not realized** .

Positive Attributes of Hope

Hope is understood more completely in context with its positive attributes. Although hope does not always result in a positive result or outcome, there are seven attributes of hope that are commonly recognized as beneficial in individual lives[270].

1) Increases Openness to Beneficial Future Outcomes

Hope broadens the heart and mind, enabling possibilities and opening the door to envisioning a better future. Hope makes it possible to think of the present day as a temporary point in life that has the potential to improve and to bring greater opportunities.

---

270 7 Reasons Why Finding Hope for the Future Is So Important." *AConsciouRethink.com.*, March 25, 2021 and found online on October 14, 2021 at 7 Reasons Why Finding Hope For The Future Is So Important (aconsciousrethink.com).

Hope makes it possible to **think of the present day** as a **temporary point** in life that **has the potential to improve** and to **bring greater opportunities**.

2) Affirms the Value of Committing Oneself to a Better Future

Hope allows a person to set goals and to identify a path to follow that requires a higher standard of personal expectations for oneself. The vision of that better future demands that an individual raise the bar of her or his personal performance to match a better world.

The **vision of that better future** demands that an individual **raise the bar of her or his personal performance** to match **a better world.**

3) Encourages Engaging in Productive Effort While Waiting

Hope inspires individuals to prepare for a better future by using time and resources to improve oneself and to develop the qualities that match the world in which one desires to live. The hope for a better future requires that a person does all that (s)he can possibly do to be ready for the world that awaits.

> The **hope** for a better future **requires that a person does all that (s)he can possibly do to be ready for the world that awaits.**

4) Provides Opportunities for Increased Self-Awareness

The process of hope and the challenges of difficulty enable individuals to reflect on that which they yearn to do, to learn, or to become. While waiting, yearning, and hoping for the fulfillment of what they desire, individuals with hope have a unique opportunity to examine themselves and to redirect their lives to fit their dream.

> The **process of hope** and **the challenges of difficulty** enable individuals to **reflect on that** which **they yearn to do, to learn,** or **to become.**

5) Enhances Feelings of Self-Efficacy and Self-Worth

As individuals endure and confront their fears, their disappointments, and their obstacles, they have the opportunity to refine and polish their lives and discover the value within themselves. The journey of hope enables every person to come to understand their courage, their capacity, and their worth.

The **journey of hope** enables every person to **come to understand** their **courage**, their **capacity**, and **their worth**.

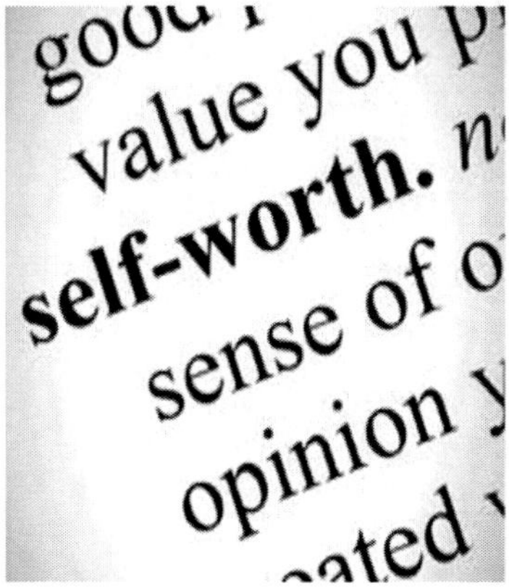

6) Promotes Positive Feelings Toward Others

As individuals engage in their own struggles in the process of enduring, they come to appreciate the courage, strength, and integrity that others show as they face their own obstacles. Having an unfulfilled hope becomes a means of recognizing the common path shared with others and enables individuals to value others more.

As individuals **engage in their own struggles** in **the process of enduring**, they come to **appreciate the courage, strength, and integrity** that **others show** as they **face their own obstacles**.

7) Improves Physical and Emotional Health

Hope can reduce stress and anxiety and quiet fear. It is a healer. As individuals experience hope, they develop more positive feelings about the future and its potential and are able to think more positively about themselves and the world that they seek to create.

Hope can reduce stress and anxiety and quiet fear. It is a healer.

Each of these positive attributes of hope are situationally contingent and dependent upon the context in which hope may be found. In the sections that follow, we identify hope's positive and negative impacts on individuals and organizations and the ways that hope can be effectively applied by leaders.

These **positive attributes of hope** are **situationally contingent** and **dependent upon the context** in which **hope may be found.**

Hope's Contribution to Leadership

As leaders seek to strengthen the hope of the members of their organizations, they also increase their members' understanding about the importance of their contribution. Increasing individual members' appreciation of those contributions can thereby increase the leader's effectiveness[271].

From **a leadership perspective**, hope is "**an activating force** that **enables people**, even when **faced with the most overwhelming obstacles**, to **envision a promising future** and to **set and pursue goals**.

From a leadership perspective, hope is "an activating force that enables people, even when faced with the most overwhelming obstacles, to envision a promising future and to set and pursue goals[272]." The following are five contributions which hope makes to enhance leadership within organizations.

1) Promotes Confidence, Enthusiasm, and Optimism

As leaders share hope for the future with the people that they lead, they build mutual commitment[273]. Hope affirms that the future will be positive and that small steps to creating a better organization can lead to positive outcomes when properly carried out.

---

[271] Helland, M. R., & Winston, B. E., (2005). "Toward a Deeper Understanding of Hope and Leadership." *Journal of Leadership and Organizational Studies*, Vol. 12, No. 2, pp. 42-54.

[272] *Ibid.*, p. 44.

[273] Helland, M. R. & Winston, B. E., (2005), *op. cit.*

Hope affirms that the future will be positive and that small steps to creating a better organization can lead to positive outcomes when properly carried out.

2) Encourages Extra Effort and Greater Commitment.

Leadership that incorporates hope and that shares aspirations for the future motivates employees to recognize the importance of their contribution to worthy outcomes[274]. In so doing, this opportunity to make a significant difference also increases employee commitment[275].

Leadership that incorporates hope and that shares aspirations for the future motivates employees to recognize the importance of their contribution to worthy outcomes.

---

[274] Ludema, J. D., Wilmot, T. B., & Srivastva, S., (1997). "Organization Hope: Reaffirming the Constructive Task of Social and Organizational Inquiry." *Human Relations*, Vol. 50, No. 8, pp. 1015-1053.

[275] Hackman J. R, & Oldham, G. R., (1976). "Motivation through the Design of Work: Test of a Theory." *Organizational Behavior and Human Performance,* Vol. 16, pp. 250-279.

3) Strengthens Perseverance in the Face of Obstacles

As leaders incorporate hope in the pursuit of difficult challenges, they strengthen the ability of team members to endure, persist, and persevere in their pursuit of organizational goals[276]. Increasing others' hope enables others to feel more dedicated in their efforts.

As leaders **incorporate hope** in the **pursuit of difficult challenges,** they **strengthen the ability** of team members to **endure, persist, and persevere** in their **pursuit of organizational goals.**

4) Gives Focus to the Importance of Desired Outcomes

As leaders strive to strengthen the ability of an organization to achieve its purpose and mission, they focus and elevate the significance of their organization's efforts[277]. Increasing this focus on the work of the organization makes the pursuit of desired outcomes increasingly important to employees.

As **leaders** strive to **strengthen the ability** of an **organization** to **achieve its purpose and mission**, they **focus and elevate** the **significance of their organization's efforts**.

[276] Carver, C. S., & Scheier, M. F. (1999). "Optimism." In C. R. Snyder (Ed.), *Coping, The Psychology of What Works*, NY: Oxford University Press, pp. 182-204.

[277] Helland, M. R. & Winston, B. E., (2005), *op. cit.*

5) Affirms That Taking the Right Actions Will Result in Success

Leaders who pay increased attention to accomplishing an organization's results strengthen the belief of team members that their efforts are consistent with the likelihood of success[278]. This increased effort to accomplish desired goals builds hope for success and increases employee confidence that what is being done is worth doing. Hope is associated with the willingness of a person to engage in positive and productive work while waiting for a desired outcome.

Leaders who pay increased **attention to accomplishing** an **organization's results** strengthen **the belief of team members** that **their efforts are consistent** with the **likelihood of success**.

The Downsides of Hope

Though hope can often inspire and motivate, it can nonetheless have its downside and those potential negatives should also be understood by the wise leader. Although the psychiatrist, Leon Seltzer, noted that hope was "inextricably woven into the fabric of human nature" and is generally perceived as "a positive, almost essential motivating force," he also identified the dangers of "false hope" as a concept that can "be harmful and sabotage[279]."

[278] *Ibid.*

[279] Seltzer, L. F., (2018). "7 Downsides of Hope." *Psychology Today*, July 25, 2018 and found online on October 15, 2021 at 7 Downsides of Hope | Psychology Today.

Though hope can often inspire and motivate, it can nonetheless **have its downside** and those **potential negatives should also be understood** by the **wise leader.**

Seltzer listed seven dangers of hope that can undermine individual performance and weaken the effectiveness of an organization[280].

1) Hope Can be an Inherently Biased Ideal

Although there are benefits to positive thinking, judgments and conclusions should be evaluated based upon logic and rationality. Unbridled idealism must also be tempered with the hard facts and leaders need to be careful in balancing challenging goals with setting unrealistic expectations.

Unbridled idealism must also be **tempered with the hard facts** and **leaders need to be careful in balancing challenging goals** with **setting unrealistic expectations**.

2) Hope Can Set Us Up for Disappointment and Defeat

When expectations are unduly realistic, disappointment and disillusionment can result and can severely undermine morale. Planning for

[280] *Ibid.*

favorable results should be combined with an identification of possible risks that may limit success. Identifying those risks in advance can make participants aware of those obstacles and can also make individuals aware of potential disappointment that may occur.

Planning for **favorable results** should be **combined with** an **identification** of **possible risks** that may **limit success**.

3) Hope Can Hamper Us from Adequately Preparing for Negative Outcomes

Although there are benefits to a flexible and positive outlook, many situations are best served by also preparing for a possible negative result. When the odds of a desired objective are particularly low, a wise leader will convey a hopeful perspective that includes a realistic response if the hoped-for event does not happen.

When the **odds of a desired objective** are **particularly low**, a **wise leader** will convey a **hopeful perspective** that **includes a realistic response** if the **hoped-for event does not happen**.

4) Hope Can be Like Prayer: Wishing for Something Rather than More Forcefully Working toward It

Hope that is ill-advised can sometimes replace advisable action and can actually be a detriment to achieving a favorable result. Hope should never become a substitute for wise decision-making and careful preparation. Although a person may believe in a kind and beneficent God, (s)he should never rely on divine help to replace personal accountability.

Although a person may **believe in a kind and beneficent God**, (s)he should **never rely on divine help** to **replace personal accountability**.

5) Hope Can Encourage You to Forfeit Personal Power and Control

Surrendering to external forces and depending entirely upon hope can result in losing perspective about the many positive things that can be done to obtain a desired outcome. Being personally accountable to make one's best effort in achieving a worthy objective can accompany hope and increase the likelihood of a favorable result.

Surrendering to external forces and **depending entirely upon hope** can result in **losing perspective** about the **many positive things** that **can be done** to **obtain a desired outcome**.

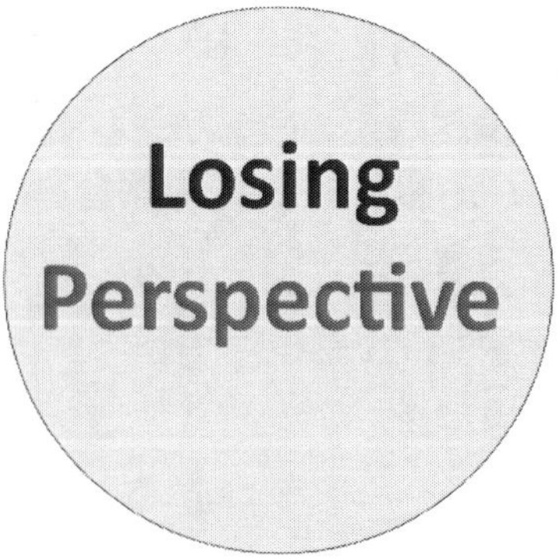

6) Hope Can Be a Tool of Self-Deception

A danger of hope is that it can be so irrational that it is self-defeating and motivate behaviors that are not in one's best interests. The self-deception involved in relying on an illogical and highly improbable hope can actually be dangerous and, when the hoped-for outcome does not occur, it can be devastating to individuals and to an organization.

The **self-deception involved** in **relying on an illogical and highly improbable hope** can actually **be dangerous** and, **when the hoped -for outcome does not occur**, it can be **devastating to individuals and to an organization**.

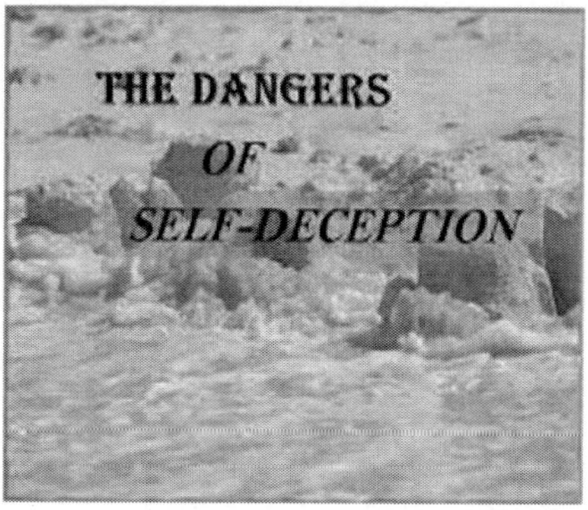

7) Hope Can Set Us Up for Hopelessness

When hope is repeatedly defeated, the outcome can be catastrophic. Despair is the absence of hope and can result in paralyzing an individual or organization. Being dependent upon hope and on a specific outcome can result in anger, resentment and the misguided decision to give up further efforts in life – including the failure to take responsibility for oneself and one's obligations.

Despair is the **absence of hope** and can result in **paralyzing** an **individual** or **organization**.

While acknowledging the benefits of hope and its universal place in life, Seltzer also advocated for a realistic assessment of likely outcomes, dedicated and focused effort, and a rational and logical perspective about all of life's possibilities[281].

Encouragement for Leaders

Understanding hope's positive attributes, its contributions to successful leadership, as well as the dangers that can come from false hope enable leaders to recognize how they can incorporate hope effectively in their relationships with others. A leader's ability to accurately assess the likelihood of positive outcomes and the most effective ways to counsel team members, can enable leaders to inspire and motivate others while reducing the likelihood of the dangers and despair that false hope can create.

A **leader's ability** to accurately **assess the likelihood of positive outcomes** and the **most effective ways to counsel team members**, can enable leaders to **inspire and motivate others** while **reducing the likelihood** of the **dangers and despair** that **false hope can create.**

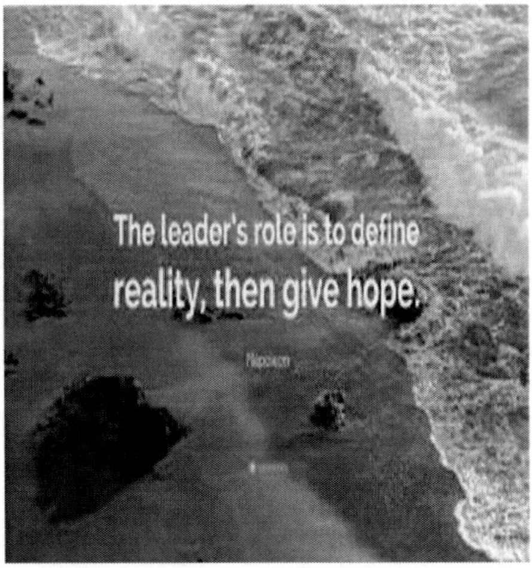

Life offers few guarantees. External factors can scuttle the best of plans. Despite these realities, hope can play a significant part in creating a culture of shared commitment and mutual partnership as organizations and team members strive to achieve the goals that they set. Leaders who recognize the attributes and characteristics of hope – including its limitations – can increase

[281] *Ibid.*

their ability to help others to be more productive, more dedicated, and more successful. Although hope is not a panacea, despite its universal role in individuals' lives, leaders who recognize its potential power and its limits can use hope appropriately to build better organizations.

Leaders who **recognize the attributes and characteristics** of hope – **including its limitations** – can **increase their ability** to **help others** to be more **productive**, more **dedicated**, and more **successful.**

References

Aquinas, T., (2012). *Summa Theologiae Prima Pars.* Dubuque, IA: Emmaus Academic, ST II-II 17.6.

Aquinas, T., (1956). *Scriptum super Sententiis.* Lethielleux-Rousteau, France: Lethielleux Publishers, SsS III, 26.

Bock, C., (2016). "Hope in Ancient Greece: Aristotle on Hope, Optimism, and Courage." April 25, 2016 and found online on October 14, 2021 at Hope in Ancient Greek: Aristotle on hope, optimism, and courage – Cherice Bock

Bloeser, C. & Stahl, T., (2017). "Hope." In E. N. Zalta, (Ed.). The Stanford Encyclopedia of Philosophy. Found online on October 14, 2021 at Author and Citation Information for "Hope" (stanford.edu).

Caldwell, C., Davis, B., and Devine, J. A., (2009). "Trust, Faith, and Betrayal: Insights from Management for the Wise Believer." *Journal of Business Ethics*, Vol. 89, Iss. 1, pp. 103-114.

Carver, C. S., & Scheier, M. F. (1999). "Optimism." In C. R. Snyder (Ed.), *Coping, The Psychology of What Works*, NY: Oxford University Press, pp. 182-204.

Descartes, R. & Moriarty, M., (2016) *The Passions of the Soul and Other Late Philosophical Writings*. Oxford, UK: Oxford University Press.

Hackman J. R, & Oldham, G. R., (1976). "Motivation through the Design of Work: Test of a Theory." *Organizational Behavior and Human Performance,* Vol. 16, pp. 250-279.

Helland, M. R., & Winston, B. E., (2005). "Toward a Deeper Understanding of Hope and Leadership." *Journal of Leadership and Organizational Studies*, Vol. 12, No. 2, pp. 42-54.

Hobbes, T. & Schneider, H. W., (2017). *Leviathan*. Boston, MA: Digireads.com Publishing, Chapter LVI.14.

Hume, David, [1738] (2007). *A Treatise of Human Nature*. In D.F. Norton and M.J. Norton (Eds.). Oxford. UK Oxford University Press.

James, W., (2015). *The Will to Believe and Other Essays in Popular Philosophy*: New York: Dover Publications.

Ludema, J. D., Wilmot, T. B., & Srivastva, S., (1997). "Organization Hope: Reaffirming the Constructive Task of Social and Organizational Inquiry." *Human Relations*, Vol. 50, No. 8, pp. 1015-1053.

Meirav, A., (2009). "The Nature of Hope." *Ratio: An International Journal of Analytic Philosophy*. Vol. 22, Iss. 2, pp. 216-233.

Seltzer, L. F., (2018). "7 Downsides of Hope." *Psychology Today*, July 25, 2018 and found online on October 15, 2021 at 7 Downsides of Hope | Psychology Today.

Spinoza, B. & Elwes, R. H. M., (2021). *Ethics*, Chapter III, p. 18.

Chapter 8

Enthusiasm as Effective Leadership

Oliver Wendell Holmes, one of the most highly-regarded and frequently-cited Supreme Court Justices in American history, wisely observed, “It’s faith in something and enthusiasm for something that makes life worth living[282].” The enthusiasm that motivates the human condition brings joy to the heart and provides a personal satisfaction that keeps people focused on accomplishing a worthy goal[283]. Enthusiasm is equated with the passion for life that inspires and provides those who possess it with both richness and exuberance.

Enthusiasm is equated with the passion for life that inspires and provides those who possess it with both richness and exuberance.

The purpose of this chapter is to define enthusiasm and identify why enthusiasm is so vital in the relationship between leaders and those whom they serve. We explain why enthusiasm plays an important role in motivating performance and in empowering those who possess it. We identify five ways that leaders can increase enthusiasm within their organizations and encourage leaders to consider the benefits of being personally enthusiastic in their relationships with others as they strive to increase their effectiveness.

---

[282] “Enthusiasm Quotes.” Goodreads.com. Found online on October 17, 2021 at Enthusiasm Quotes (360 quotes) (goodreads.com).

[283] Greerson, R. R., (1962). “On Enthusiasm.” *Journal of the American Psychological Association*, Vol. 10, pp. 3-21.

Enthusiasm plays **an important role** in **motivating performance** and in **empowering those** who **possess it.**

Understanding Enthusiasm

The etymology of enthusiasm has its roots in the Greek. Enthusiasm is derived from three Greek words: ἐν or en, meaning "in or within;" θεός, or theos, meaning "god;" and οὐσία, or ousia, meaning "essence[284]." Literally, enthusiasm originally referred to the essence of god within someone. The term evolved to mean "inspiration or possession by a god." According to the *Merriam Webster Dictionary*, the term entered the English language at the beginning of the 17th Century and originally was used to refer to passionate beliefs associated with religion[285]. More commonly today, enthusiasm refers to strong or intense positive feelings akin to excitement about an idea, an opportunity, a situation, or an event[286].

Napoleon Hill has stated that "Enthusiasm is fueled by inspiration and perseverance, travels with passion, and its destination is excellence[287]." Enthusiasm is known for its ability to lighten every effort and turn difficult labor into pleasant work[288].

---

[284] Oxford University Press, (2008). *The Oxford New Greek Dictionary: The Essential Resource Revised and Updated*. New York: Berkley Publishing.

[285] Merriam-Webster Online Dictionary. "Enthusiasm." Found online on October 17, 2021 at Enthusiasm | Definition of Enthusiasm by Merriam-Webster.

[286] Peale, N. V., (2003). *Enthusiasm Makes the Difference*. New York: Touchstone.

[287] "Napoleon Hill Quotes Success." *Bing.com*. Found online on October 18, 2021 at napoleon hill quotes success - Bing images.

[288] "James Baldwin Quotes." *Goodreads.com*. Found online on October 18, 2021 at James Baldwin Quotes (Author of Giovanni's Room) (goodreads.com).

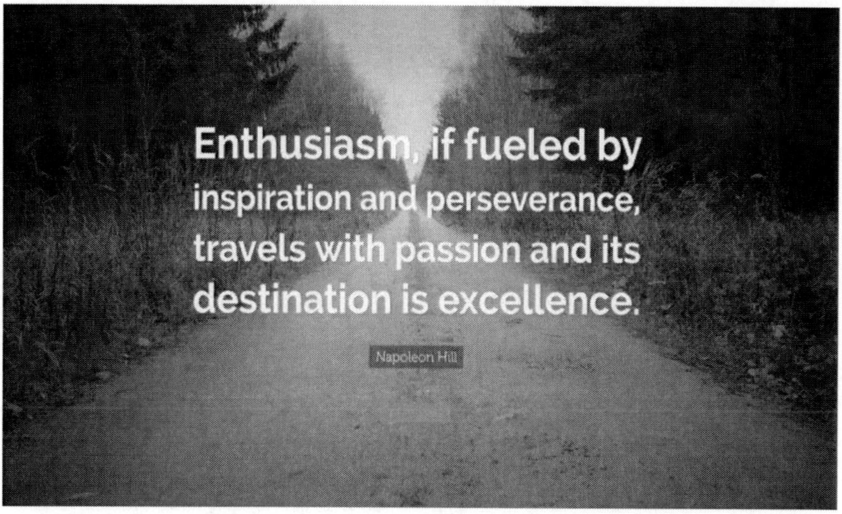

Ralph R. Greerson, who has written a comprehensive paper about enthusiasm, defines it as follows[289].

> Enthusiasm is a happy and joyous state of mind. It is a condition of high spirits—a special form of elation. Enthusiasm has some of the buoyancy of euphoria and the activity of mania, and it is obviously different from blissful and peaceful elations...There is an air of extravagance and expansiveness about enthusiasm—a readiness to use superlatives. The enthusiastic person does not feel good or even very good, but great—in fact, the "greatest." There is a sense of exuberance, richness, an abundance of good fortune; yet with it all, there is some awareness that one is exaggerating; but it is enjoyable and one is reluctant to give it up.

In his review of the nature of enthusiasm, Greerson has compared it to many related terms while distinguishing it from other concepts. The following are examples of his description.

---

289 Greerson, R. R., (1962), op. cit., p. 3.

Generosity

Enthusiasm motivates a person to "share his richness with others[290]."

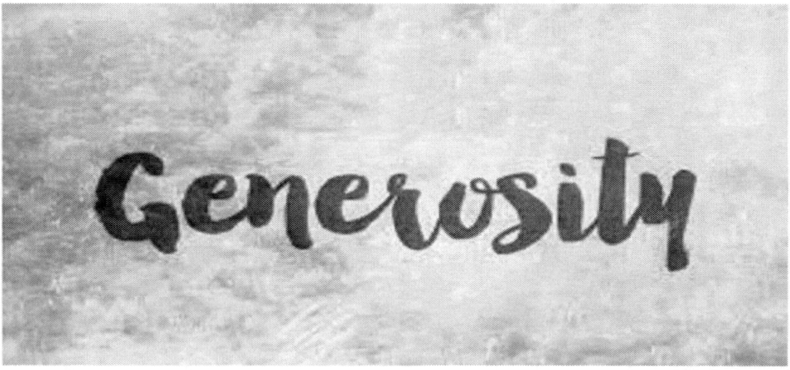

Positivity

"To be enthused means being filled with goodness as opposed to the feeling full of badness and the feeling full of emptiness as in boredom[291]."

---

[290] *Ibid.*, p. 4.
[291] *Ibid.*, p. 4.

Fragility

Enthusiasm is fragile and vulnerable and lack of response can smother it[292].

Temporary

Prolonged enthusiasm may be "neurotic or hypomania[293]."

Contagious

Enthusiasm felt by one person is often felt by others[294].

292 *Ibid.*, p. 4.
293 *Ibid.*, p. 4.
294 *Ibid.*, p. 4.

Leadership Inclined

Enthusiasm is one of the most valuable characteristics in determining leadership potential[295].

Creativity-Promoting

Enthusiasm promotes constructive and adaptive responses to problems[296]

---

295 *Ibid.*, p. 4.
296 *Ibid.*, p. 5.

Image-Enhancing

Enthusiasm can influence a person's self-confidence and self-image[297].

Image Enhancing

Each of these qualities associated with enthusiasm can be of benefit to individuals who possess the quality, as well as the organizations with which they are associated.

Enthusiasm, Leadership, and Performance

Ralph Waldo Emerson famously stated, "Nothing great was ever achieved without enthusiasm[298]." He added, "When you do a thing, do it with all your might. Put your whole soul into it. Stamp it with your personality. Be active, be energetic, be enthusiastic and faithful, and you will accomplish your objective[299]." Enthusiastic leaders substantially affect performance by the commitment that they show to achieve meaningful goals. Leaders frequently show their enthusiasm in several ways[300].

Keep Curiosity Alive

Leaders constantly look for new and more effective ways to accomplish goals and set the example for others to follow.

---

[297] *Ibid.*, pp. 5-6.

[298] "Ralph Waldo Emerson Quotes." *A-Z Quotes.com*. Found online on October 18, 2021 at TOP 25 QUOTES BY RALPH WALDO EMERSON (of 4214) | A-Z Quotes (azquotes.com).

[299] *Ibid.*

[300] *Managing People at Work*, (2020). "Your Enthusiasm is the Leadership Key." May 15, 2020, Vol. 7, Iss. 10.

Own Ambition

Leaders focus their ambition and on achieving good results and don't feel guilty about it. They encourage colleagues at work to achieve their ambitions as well.

Being Flexible

Leaders have the ability to change strategies and to adapt to changing conditions. They involve employees and make them an active part of the change process.

Staying in Touch

Leaders talk about their passion for working with others and encourage those with whom they work to do the same. Leaders use others' feedback to then make their jobs more fulfilling and satisfying.

IN TOUCH

By their personal examples, leaders are able to demonstrate their commitment to both the success of their organizations and the colleagues with whom they work[301]. Building enthusiasm is most effective by making others full partners and active contributors to successes that are achieved[302]. Enthusiasm has been called the key to the difference between success and failure and the key to accomplishing something remarkable in life[303].

Enthusiasm has been called **the key to the difference between success and failure** and **the key to accomplishing something remarkable** in life.

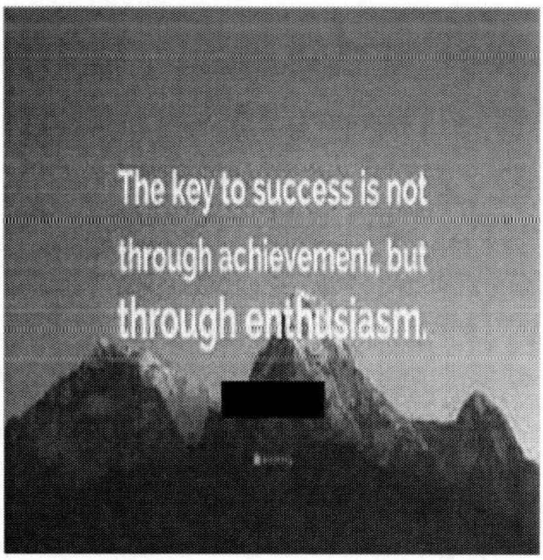

---

[301] *Ibid.*

[302] Block, P., (2013). *Stewardship: Choosing Service Over Self-Interest*. San Francisco, CA: Jossey-Bass.

[303] Peale, N. V., (2003), *op. cit.*

Leadership and Building Enthusiasm

Anita Campbell, a small business entrepreneur and author, has suggested five important ways for leaders to build enthusiasm in the workplace and injecting energy into those with whom they labor[304].

1) Go Beyond Skills

Although technical skills are important, great employees have heart and the will to succeed. Such individuals not only never give up but they encourage others as well. Praise heart when you see it and develop heart within yourself and in others on your team.

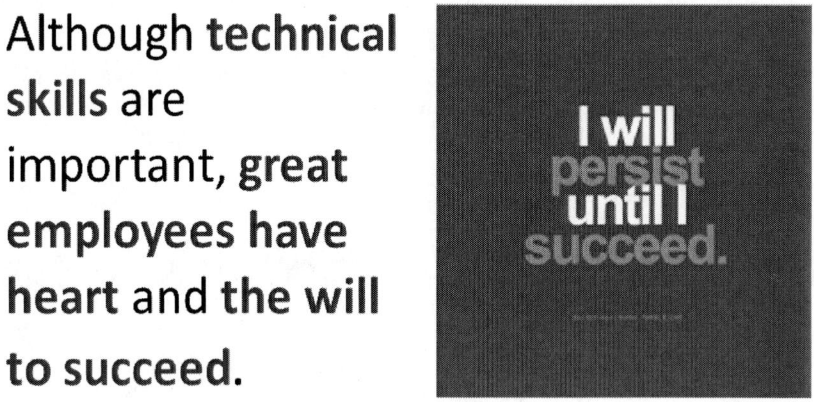

2) Appeal to Passions

Passions are about how people feel about what they do and what they are trying to accomplish. Emotions are ultimately what achieve meaningful results. Learn what appeals to individuals in your organization and encourage them. People who buy in to enthusiasm accomplish great things.

[304] Campbell, A., (2019). "5 Ways to Build Enthusiasm at Work."

Learn what appeals to individuals in your organization and encourage them. People who buy in to enthusiasm accomplish great things.

3) Celebrate Accomplishments – Small and Large

Nothing breeds success within an organization like an environment of success and recognizing both small and major achievements help to create that environment. Point out successes of members of your team and include your own accomplishments as well. Highlight your accomplishments and express appreciation to those whose efforts brought them about.

Point out successes of members of your team and include your own.

4) Be Playful

Make work enjoyable and fun. Work means more to individuals when their associates are also their friends. When people care about each other, they are more committed and look forward to their interactions with their colleagues. Make work an enjoyable place to be and people will work harder and work more effectively.

Make work an enjoyable place to be and people will work harder and work more effectively.

5) Do Something Unexpected

Leaders create pleasant surprises for the members of their organizations and treat them as valued partners. They focus on creating goodwill with the people with whom they work and acknowledge others' uniqueness and value. Leaders look for opportunities to let people know that they are not only appreciated but cared about.

Look for opportunities to let people know that they are not only appreciated but cared about.

The great value of enthusiasm is that it is a personal, emotional, and completely human way of conveying to others that they are "yous" and not "its" – and that their leaders are human, humane, and caring. Communicating to people that they matter and that their contributions to an organization are taken seriously builds an *esprit* and sense of mutual commitment that inspires and motivates.

The **great value of enthusiasm** is that it is a **personal, emotional, and completely human** way of **conveying to others that they are "yous" and not "its"** – and that **their leaders are human, humane, and caring.**

APPRECIATING

THE VALUE

OF

ENTHUSIASM

The Challenge to Leaders

The North Carolina State basketball coach, Jim Valvano, understood the great value of goals – understanding where you are, where you want to be, and how to get there. He said, "I think you have to have enthusiasm for life. You have to have a dream, a goal. And you have to be willing to work for it[305]."

[305] "Jim Valvano Quotes." A-Z Quotes.com. Found online on October 18, 2021 at TOP 25 QUOTES BY JIM VALVANO (of 52) | A-Z Quotes (azquotes.com).

That appreciation of the importance of something great to achieve in life and the passion to pursue that goal was also shared by George Bernard Shaw. In his play, "Arms and the Man," the character articulates Shaw's insights about life.

> This is the true joy in life, being used for a purpose recognized by yourself as a mighty one. Being a force of nature instead of a feverish, selfish little clod of ailments and grievances complaining that the world will not devote itself to making you happy. I am of the opinion that my life belongs to the whole community and as I live it is my privilege – my *privilege* to do for it whatever I can. I want to be thoroughly used up when I die, for the harder I work the more I love. I rejoice in life for its own sake. Life is no brief candle to me; it is a sort of splendid torch which I've got a hold of for the moment and I want to make it burn as brightly as possible before handing it on to future generations.

As leaders come to appreciate the importance of achieving great goals, they achieve that "true joy in life about which Shaw described. Great dreams and great deeds are achieved with enthusiasm and with the passion, commitment, and dedication that it drives. Those who wish to wear the mantle of leadership must be prepared to commit themselves with enthusiasm to achieving that which is truly important.

Great dreams and great deeds are **achieved with enthusiasm** and with **the passion, commitment, and dedication** that it drives.

References

A-Z Quotes.com. Found online on October 18, 2021 at TOP 25 QUOTES BY JIM VALVANO (of 52) | A-Z Quotes (azquotes.com).

Block, P., (2013). *Stewardship: Choosing Service Over Self-Interest.* San Francisco, CA: Jossey-Bass.

Campbell, A., (2019). "5 Ways to Build Enthusiasm at Work."

Greerson, R. R., (1962). "On Enthusiasm." *Journal of the American Psychological Association*, Vol. 10, pp. 3-21.

Managing People at Work, (2020). "Your Enthusiasm is the Leadership Key." May 15, 2020, Vol. 7, Iss. 10.

Merriam-Webster Online Dictionary. "Enthusiasm." Found online on October 17, 2021 at Enthusiasm | Definition of Enthusiasm by Merriam-Webster.

Oxford University Press, (2008). *The Oxford New Greek Dictionary: The Essential Resource Revised and Updated.* New York: Berkley Publishing.

Peale, N. V., (2003). *Enthusiasm Makes the Difference.* New York: Touchstone.

Chapter 9

Ethical Stewardship as Quiet Passion

In the quest for sustaining effective leadership, leaders recognize the importance of earning the trust and followership of members of their organizations. Personal credibility is earned by leaders as they demonstrate their ability to be perceived as being personally trustworthy – the integration of character, competence, capacity, clarity, and caring[306]. Leaders of all types are expected to meet their responsibilities as stewards who seek to honor obligations due to all stakeholders while optimizing their ability to generate profits for their organizations[307].

Personal credibility is earned by leaders as they demonstrate their ability to be perceived as being personally trustworthy – the integration of character, competence, capacity, clarity, and caring.

The focus of this chapter is on the role of ethical stewards who quietly but passionately lead organizations as they assist those with whom they labor. We begin the chapter by explaining stewardship theory and differentiate it from agency and stakeholder theories. We describe the unique strengths of ethical stewardship as a leadership model and identify eight principles upon which ethical stewardship is based. We conclude the chapter by encouraging those

---

[306] Caldwell, C., and Ndalamba, K. K., (2017). "Trust and Being 'Worthy' – The Keys to Creating Wealth." *Journal of Management Development*, Vol. 36, Iss. 8, pp. 1076-1086.

[307] Caldwell, C. & Anderson, V., (2019). "Stewardship as a Transformative Model." In C. Caldwell & V. Anderson (Eds.), *Trust, Trustworthiness, and Stewardship: A Transformative Approach*. Hauppauge, New York: NOVA Publishing, Chapter 5.

who lead to adopt the principles of ethical stewardship as they work within their organizations.

Understanding Ethical Stewardship

Stewardship Theory is a theory of organizational governance in which those who lead are stewards of the interests of multiple parties who have an interest in the organization and its achievements[308]. Stewardship Theory distinguishes itself from other theories of governance by its perspective about the importance of long-term wealth creation.

Stewardship Theory is a **theory of organizational governance** in which **those who lead are stewards of the interests of multiple parties** who **have an interest** in the **organization and its achievements.**

In contrast to Stewardship Theory, historically the leader has been asked to honors the responsibility to those who own the company or who are shareholders/investors to ensure that the organization is optimally profitable over the short term. Although agents are supposed to be "morally responsible to maximize shareholder utility," their financial interests may sometimes diverge from that of the principals because of contractual incentives in their relationship[309]. The underlying assumption of Agency Theory is that the agent is economically motivated to pursue her/his own economic self-interest[310].

[308] Davis, J. H., Schoorman, F. D. & Donaldson, L., (1997). "Toward a Stewardship Theory of Management." *Academy of Management Review*, Vol. 22, No. 1, pp. 20–47.
[309] *Ibid.*, p. 22.
[310] *Ibid.*

Although **agents are** supposed to be "**morally responsible to maximize shareholder utility,**" their **financial interests may sometimes diverge** from that of **the principals** because of **contractual incentives** in their relationship. The **underlying assumption of Agency Theory** is that the **agent is economically motivated** to pursue **her/his own economic self-interest**.

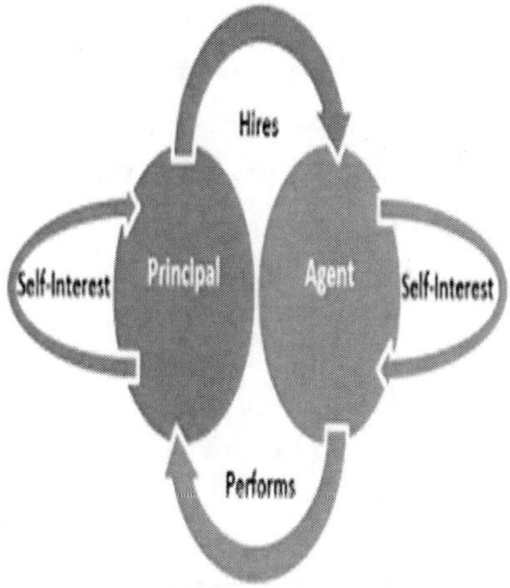

Davis and colleagues explain the assumptions of Stewardship Theory as follows.

> In stewardship theory, the model of man is based on a steward whose behavior is ordered such that pro-organizational, collectivistic behaviors have higher utility than individualistic, self-serving behaviors. Given a choice between self-serving behavior and pro-organizational behavior, a steward's behavior will not depart from the interests of his or her organization. A steward will not substitute or trade self-serving behaviors for cooperative behaviors…Because the steward perceives greater utility in cooperative behavior and behaves accordingly, his or her behavior can be considered rational[311].

The distinguishing difference between the agent and the steward is that the agent's interests can be extrinsically focused on financial self-interest while the steward is intrinsically driven to achieve the best possible result for the organization[312].

---

[311] *Ibid.*, p. 24.
[312] *Ibid.*

The **distinguishing difference** between the **agent and the steward** is that the **agent's interests can be extrinsically focused on financial self-interest** while the **steward is intrinsically driven** to achieve the **best possible result for the organization**.

Ethical Stewardship is based upon that assumption that the most effective organizational leader is one who seeks to optimize the long-term financial best interests of the principal/shareholders while honoring the obligations due to other key organizational stakeholders[313]. Ethical Stewardship acknowledges that all of an organization's stakeholders play a key role in the profitability of an organization. However, while Stakeholder Theory seeks to reconcile and balance the potential conflicts of interest that exist between stakeholders, Ethical Stewardship takes the position that those interests are aligned when considered from a long-term perspective[314].

Ethical Stewardship is based upon that **assumption that the most effective organizational leader** is one who **seeks to optimize the long-term financial best interests** of the **principal/shareholders while honoring the obligations due to other key organizational stakeholders**

[313] Caldwell, C., Hayes, L., Karri, R., & Bernal, P., (2008). "Ethical Stewardship: Implications for Leadership and Trust." *Journal of Business Ethics*, Vol. 78, Iss. 1/2, pp. 153-164.

[314] *Ibid.*

Ethical Stewardship focuses on the leader's role as balancing normative values of an organization with the instrumental objectives of goal accomplishment – but takes the position that outcomes are most effectively achieved when people are treated as valued partners who have a shared interest in an organization's success. Rather than focusing on sub-optimizing the achievement of results by compromising long-term priorities, Ethical Stewardship seeks to optimize long-term results in the interest of all stakeholders[315].

Ethical Stewardship focuses on the **leader's role as balancing normative values** of an organization **with the instrumental objectives of goal accomplishment**– but takes the position that **outcomes are most effectively achieved when people are treated as valued partners** who have a **shared interest in an organization's success**

Principles of Ethical Stewardship

Ethical Stewardship is best accomplished "when leaders earn the trust and followership of those whom they serve by creating integrated organizational systems that demonstrate the leader's commitment to honoring the steward's duties[316]." As a virtue-based model of leadership, Ethical Stewardship emphasizes a commitment to eight ethically-based principles that enable leaders to guide their organizations in the pursuit of best possible outcomes.

[315] *Ibid.*
[316] *Ibid.*, p. 157.

Leadership Relationships Are Dyadic One-on-One Partnerships

The focus of Ethical Stewardship is on personal relationships. Such leaders care about each member of their organizations and demonstrate that by their commitment to each employee's welfare and wellbeing. Employees are engaged and empowered partners in contributing to its successes.

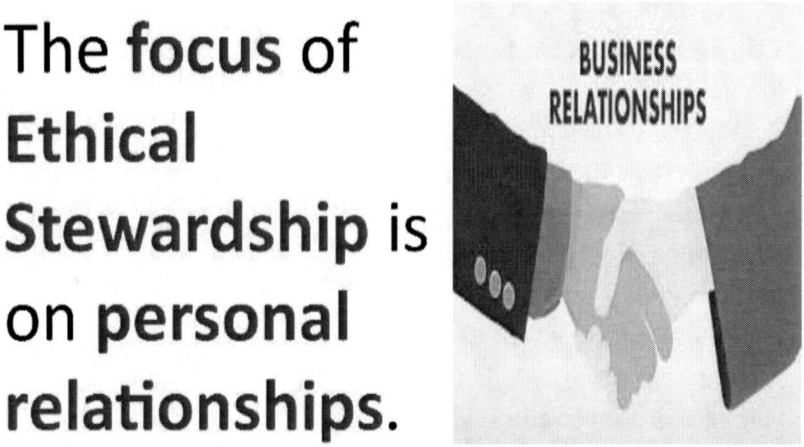

1) Investing in Constant Learning is the Key to Continuous Improvement

In honoring their commitment to employees' interests, Ethical Stewards seek to develop employees at all levels of the organization and emphasize constant learning to enable the organization to evolve and excel[317]. Constant learning and continuous improvement are essential in developing the high-trust and high-performance culture upon which Ethical Stewardship is based[318].

[317] Caldwell, C., Truong, D., Linh, P., and Tuan, A., (2011). "Strategic Human Resource Management as Ethical Stewardship." *Journal of Business Ethics*, Vol. 98, Iss. 1., pp. 171-182.

[318] Beer, M., (2009). *High Commitment High Performance: How to Build a Resilient Organization for Sustained Advantage*. San Francisco, CA: Jossey-Bass.

Constant learning and continuous improvement are essential in developing the high-trust and high-performance culture upon which Ethical Stewardship is based.

2) Organizational Purpose and Values Drive Participant Commitment

Ethical Stewardship emphasizes achieving an important organizational purpose and is mission driven[319]. Its commitment to clearly defined values drives employee involvement and ownership[320]. The most effective leaders earn trust as they honor organization values and set the example – but do so in an understated way that focuses on the organization's achievements rather than their own[321].

Ethical Stewardship emphasizes achieving an important organizational purpose and is mission driven. Its commitment to clearly defined values drives employee involvement and ownership.

---

319 Caldwell, C, Hayes, L., Karri, R. & Bernal, P., (2008), *op. cit.*

320 *Ibid.*

321 Collins, J., (2001). *Good to Great: Why Some Companies Make the Leap . . . And Others Don't.* New York: HarperCollins.

3) Relationships Established are Transformational and Transactional

Transformational relationships are intrinsic and acknowledge an organization's responsibility to help employees grow and progress[322]. Transactional relationships involve a quid pro quo extrinsic exchange and for employees that exchange typically includes compensation for work performed – including appropriate incentives for excellence in achievements[323]. Ethical Stewardship creates both transformational and transactional relationships with employees[324].

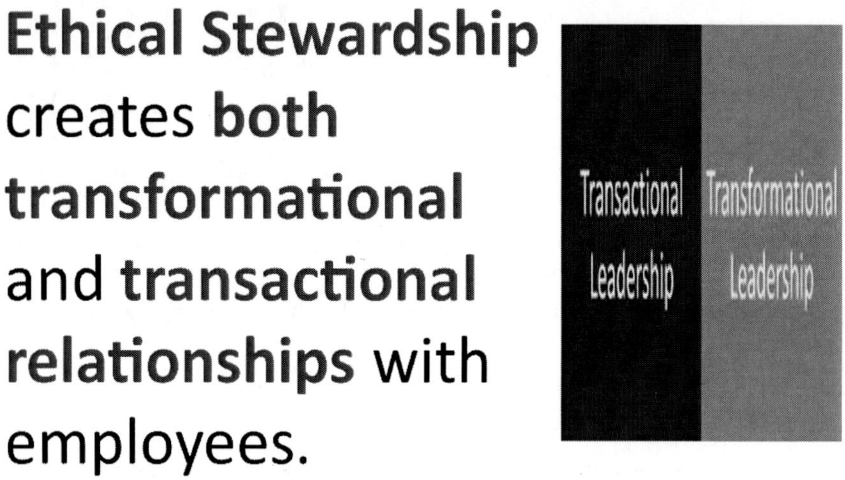

4) Decision-Making Seeks to Carefully Manage Risks and Opportunities

The decision process of Ethical Stewardship carefully considers risks and the pursuit of outcomes that create the greatest long-term value for organizations. Ethical Stewards avoid high risk options that can undermine the ability of an organization to be successful. Decisions that involve risk are most effective when carefully planned and incrementally tested before being adopted organization-wide[325].

---

322 Caldwell, C, Hayes, L., Karri, R. & Bernal, P., (2008), *op. cit.*
323 *Ibid.*
324 *Ibid.*
325 Collins, J. & Hansen, M. T., (2011). *Great by Choice: Uncertainty, Chaos, and Luck—Why Some Thrive Despite Them All.* New York: HarperCollins.

The decision process of Ethical Stewardship carefully considers risks and the pursuit of outcomes that create the greatest long-term value for organizations.

5) Relationships Honor Implicit and Explicit Psychological Contracts

Psychological contracts are the implicit and explicit expectations that are individually held by employees in the relationships that are established between employees and the organization[326]. Ethical Stewardship is highly committed to honoring obligations owed to employees and the focus of communication is intended to clarify social contract expectations[327].

Psychological contracts are the implicit and explicit expectations that are individually held by employees in the relationships that are established between employees and the organization.

---

[326] Rousseau, D. M., (1995). *Psychological Contracts in Organizations: Understanding Written and Unwritten Agreements*. Thousand Oaks, CA: Sage Publications.

[327] Caldwell, C, Hayes, L., Karri, R. & Bernal, P., (2008), *op. cit.*

6) Communication is Constant and Emphasizes the Management of Meaning

The focus of Ethical Stewardship is on two-way communication and emphasizes the important of creating healthy partnerships that empower all members[328]. Ethical Stewardship emphasizes listening to and empowering employees in the process of making them partners in achieving organization goals[329]. Values are communicated by creating aligned organizational systems – emphasizing actions rather than just words[330].

Ethical Stewardship emphasizes **listening to and empowering employees** in the **process of making them partners** in achieving **organization goals.**

7) The Focus of Outcomes is Both Short-Term and Long-Term

Ethical Stewardship acknowledges that stakeholder needs must be addressed both short-term but must also achieve solutions that optimize long-term wealth creation and that benefit all stakeholders thereby[331]. Decisions made are ethically justified and communicated to employees to clarify how stakeholders are affected by decision choices in order to explain the decision process and its rationale[332].

---

[328] Caldwell, C., Truong, D., Linh, P., and Tuan, A., (2011), *op. cit.*

[329] *Ibid.*

[330] Pfeffer, J., (1998). *The Human Equation: Building Profits by Putting People First*. Boston, MA: Harvard Business Review Press.

[331] Caldwell, C, Hayes, L., Karri, R. & Bernal, P., (2008), *op. cit.*

[332] Hosmer. L. T., (2010). *The Ethics of Management* (7th Ed.). Boston, MA: McGraw-Hill Education.

Decisions made are **ethically justified** and **communicated** to employees **to clarify how stakeholders are affected** by decision choices in order **to explain the decision** process and **its rationale**.

By incorporating these eight principles, Ethical Stewards create organizational cultures that reinforce their personal dedication, example, and commitment to excellence. Relationships created with employees throughout an organization reinforce the values espoused by their leader and communicate a clear message that reinforces the organizational systems that match leadership principles[333].

Relationships created with employees **throughout an organization reinforce** the **values espoused by their leader** and **communicate a clear message** that **reinforces the organizational systems** that **match leadership principles**.

[333] Schein, E. H. & Schein, P. A., (2016). *Organizational Culture and Leadership* (5th ed.). San Francisco, CA: Jossey-Bass.

Encouragement to Leaders

As leaders in modern organizations struggle to be perceived as worthy of others' trust, the challenges that they commonly face are often ethically-based. In today's chaotic and competitive world, the demands placed on leaders to cut corners, treat employees like commodities, and pursue short-term priorities are all pressures that make a leader's job difficult. Despite these challenges, the cost to leaders of compromising correct principles for expedient solutions is not the answer if those leaders are to be perceived as worthy of others' respect and commitment[334].

In today's chaotic and competitive world, the **demands** placed on leaders to **cut corners, treat employees like commodities,** and **pursue short-term priorities** are all **pressures** that **make a leader's job difficult.**

Although Ethical Stewards are not high profile or self-promoting, this leadership approach earns others' followership and by the leader's commitment to the organizations' success and employees' growth[335]. Quietly but with a passionate commitment to excellence, Ethical Stewards demonstrate their dedication by creating systems and processes that empower employees and unlock their potential[336].

---

334 Caldwell, C., and Ndalamba, K. K., (2017), *op. cit.*
335 Caldwell, C. & Anderson, V., (2019), *op. cit.*
336 Pfeffer, J., (1998), *op. cit.*

Quietly but with a passionate commitment to excellence, Ethical Stewards demonstrate their dedication by creating systems and processes that empower employees and unlock their potential.

Ethical Stewardship's alignment with correct principles and its commitment to others' wellbeing enables leaders who adopt its concepts to unlock the potential of employees that so often goes undeveloped – but that is the key to long-term profitability and organizational sustainability[337]. Although the principles of Ethical Stewardship set a high standard for leaders, the return that comes from honoring those standards is worth the effort.

References

Beer, M., (2009). High Commitment High Performance: How to Build a Resilient Organization for Sustained Advantage. San Francisco, CA: Jossey-Bass.

Caldwell, C. & Anderson, V., (2019). "Stewardship as a Transformative Model." In C. Caldwell & V. Anderson (Eds.), Trust, Trustworthiness, and Stewardship: A Transformative Approach. Hauppauge, New York: NOVA Publishing, Chapter 5.

Caldwell, C., and Ndalamba, K. K., (2017). "Trust and Being 'Worthy' – The Keys to Creating Wealth." Journal of Management Development, Vol. 36, Iss. 8, pp. 1076-1086

Caldwell, C., Truong, D., Linh, P., and Tuan, A., (2011). "Strategic Human Resource Management as Ethical Stewardship." Journal of Business Ethics, Vol. 98, Iss. 1., pp. 171-182.

Caldwell, C., Hayes, L., Karri, R., & Bernal, P., (2008). "Ethical Stewardship: Implications for Leadership and Trust." Journal of Business Ethics, Vol. 78, Iss. 1/2, pp. 153-164.

Collins, J. & Hansen, M. T., (2011). Great by Choice: Uncertainty, Chaos, and Luck—Why Some Thrive Despite Them All. New York: HarperCollins.

---

[337] Covey, S. R., (1992). *Principle-Centered Leadership*. New York: Touchstone Books.

Collins, J., (2001). Good to Great: Why Some Companies Make the Leap . . . And Others Don't. New York: HarperCollins.

Covey, S. R., (1992). Principle-Centered Leadership. New York: Touchstone Books.

Davis, J. H., Schoorman, F. D. & Donaldson, L., (1997). "Toward a Stewardship Theory of Management." Academy of Management Review, Vol. 22, No. 1, pp. 20–47.

Hosmer. L. T., (2010). The Ethics of Management (7th Ed.). Boston, MA: McGraw-Hill Education.

Pfeffer, J., (1998). The Human Equation: Building Profits by Putting People First. Boston, MA: Harvard Business Review Press.

Rousseau, D. M., (1995). Psychological Contracts in Organizations: Understanding Written and Unwritten Agreements. Thousand Oaks, CA: Sage Publications.

Schein, E. H. & Schein, P. A., (2016). Organizational Culture and Leadership (5th ed.). San Francisco, CA: Jossey-Bass.

Chapter 10

Leading with Passion and Self-Control

Passion both motivates a person to do what (s)he loves and inspires that person to do something extraordinary. People invest in that upon which they place value, are actively engaged, and find joy in accomplishments when pursuing a goal associated with an activity that they love[338]. Passion can consume human interests, enable individuals to excel, achieve unprecedented heights, and exceed the expectations of others as well as of themselves[339].

Passion can consume human interests, enable individuals to excel, achieve unprecedented heights, and exceed the expectations of others as well as of themselves.

The purpose of this chapter is to identify the complex nature of passion as an inspiring quality of leaders but to emphasize the importance of passion being something that positively contributes to an individual's life, growth, and effectiveness with others. We begin the chapter by defining passion as a motivational force that drives individuals in the pursuit of a desired objective. We distinguish between obsessive and harmonious passion and note that

---

[338] Vallerand, R. J. & Houlfort, N (2003). "Passion at Work: Toward a New Conceptualization." In S. W. Gilliland, D. D. Steiner & D. P. Skarlicki (Eds.). *Emerging Perspectives on Values in Organizations*. Greenwich, CN: Information Age Publishing, pp. 175-204.

[339] *Ibid.*

passion can have positive and negative implications for individuals. We identify the relationship between passions and the individual identity and offer six suggestions for leaders to help them to assess the ways in which they monitor themselves, and control their emotions as they express their passion in the leadership role. The chapter concludes with a challenge to leaders to apply these suggestions as they integrate passion and self-control in interacting with others.

Understanding the Nature of Passion

Passion is a powerful emotional force that drives human actions. The derivation of the word comes from the Latin *pati* and its nominative form *passio*[340]. The word meant "to endure, to undergo, and to experience" and came to refer to suffering or "that which must be endured[341]." In defining the word, the dictionary notes that "the distinctive mark of passion is that it masters the mind, so that the person becomes seemingly its subject or its passive instrument[342]."

Passion can be **directed toward an activity** but also **toward objects, causes, ideals or beliefs,** and **other people.** Passion, in fact, can **permeate virtually every aspect of life** from **politics** to **business** and from **sports** to **science.**

From a practical perspective, passion can be directed toward an activity but also toward objects, causes, ideals or beliefs, and other people[343]. Passion,

[340] Online Etymology Dictionary. "Passion." Found online on October 27, 2021 at https://www.etymonline.com/word/passion.

[341] *Ibid.*

[342] *Ibid.*

[343] Vallerand, R. J., (2015). *The Psychology of Passion: A Dualistic Model*. Oxford, UK: Oxford University Press.

in fact, can permeate virtually every aspect of life from politics to business and from sports to science[344]. It is also well recognized that passion can generate both positive devotion and feelings but also intense negative feelings that can be disruptive and counterproductive[345]. Accordingly, passion has the power to become a compelling quality that an individual must both understand and control if it is to be productively utilized[346].

Although passion associated with the love of participating in an activity is frequently cited, such passion may actually be dysfunctional in its impact.

Although passion associated with the love of participating in an activity is frequently cited, such passion may actually be dysfunctional in its impact[347]. In their insightful review of the nature of passion, Vallerand and Houlfort proposed that there are two distinctive types of passion. They identify obsessive passion as a motivational force that compels or controls a person in a specific way – as in being compelled to engage in an activity or feel compelled to devote oneself to a task[348].

The obsessive devotion to an activity or task may begin to play such a dominant role that it gets out of balance with the healthy purposes of a person's life and may disproportionately define a person's identity[349]. In contrast, a harmonious passion activity is in harmony with other aspects of a person's life and does not become disproportionately important or work in conflict with other priorities[350]. The distinction for a harmonious passion versus an

---

[344] *Ibid.*

[345] *Ibid.*

[346] Vallerand, R. J. & Houlfort, N., (2003), *op. cit.*

[347] Vallerand, R. J., (2015), *op. cit.*

[348] Vallerand, R. J. & Houlfort, N., (2003), *op. cit.*, p. 178.

[349] *Ibid.*

[350] *Ibid.*

obsessive passion is the degree to which an activity or task is valued and the extent which engagement in the activity is internalized as a part of the identity that compels a person to action[351].

The distinction for a harmonious passion versus an obsessive passion is the degree to which an activity or task is valued and the extent which engagement in the activity is internalized as a part of the identity that compels a person to action.

OBSESSIVE PASSION

and

HARMONIOUS PASSION

With obsessive passion, the failure to perform a task successfully can become a detriment to how a person values herself or himself and can undermine feelings of personal self-worth, disappointment, and depression[352]. This obsessive passion can lead to choices that are out of proportion with the more important values that are central to a person's identity[353]. Obsessive passions can distort perceptions of reality, fog clear thinking and thwart the achievement of more important priorities, restrict personal development, and impede long-term growth or good health, and seriously undermine good judgment that can result in inappropriate emotional and intellectual responses[354].

---

[351] Ibid., p. 178-179.
[352] *Ibid.*
[353] *Ibid.*
[354] *Ibid.*

Obsessive passions can distort perceptions of reality, fog clear thinking and thwart the achievement of more important priorities, restrict personal development, and impede long-term growth or good health, and seriously undermine good judgment that can result in inappropriate emotional and intellectual responses

Obsessive Passion Distorts Reality

Where harmonious passion tends to produce increased focus and improved performance, obsessive passion can produce anxiety, frustration, dysfunctional task performance, and negative emotional responses[355]. Harmonious passion and obsessive passion both have been found to be predictors of tasks and activities, but harmonious passion generated subjective wellbeing while obsessive passion was likely to produce unrelated or negatively related feelings about subjective wellbeing[356]. Harmonious passion also resulted in an increase in work satisfaction and a decrease in work conflicts while obsessive passion increased both work conflict and feelings of burnout[357].

---

355 Vallerand, R. J., Salvy, S.-J., Mageau, G. A., Elliot, A. J., Denis, P. L., Grouzet, F. M. E. & Blanchard, C., (2007). "On the Role of Passion in Performance." *Journal of Personality*, Vol. 75, Iss. 3, pp. 505-534.

356 *Ibid.*

357 Vallerand, R. J. Paquet, Y. Fillipe, F. L. & Charest, J., (2010). On the Role of Passion for Work in Burnout: A Process Model." *Journal of Personality*, Vol. 78, Iss. 1, pp. 289-312.

Harmonious passion leads to **constructive achievement of shared goals** and **greater satisfaction with outcomes**. **Obsessive passion** can lead to **inflexible thinking, rigid persistence,** and **illogical behavior** that can literally **destroy relationships, burn bridges,** and **undermine long-term success.**

In relationships, passion can generate strong negative emotions and anger. With regard to passion in relationships, with harmonious passion, the passion is under the control of the individual but with obsessive passion, the passion controls the person[358]. Harmonious passion leads to constructive achievement of shared goals and greater satisfaction with outcomes. Obsessive passion can lead to inflexible thinking, rigid persistence, and illogical behavior that can literally destroy relationships, burn bridges, and undermine long-term success[359].

Passion and the Identity

As individuals seek to effectively incorporate passion in their lives, they can increase that ability as they expand their awareness of their personal identities. The identity has been described as the set of social roles that a person plays and their perceptions about how those roles and associated values guide their choices.

---

[358] Vallerand, R. J. & Carbonneau, N., (2016). "The Role of Passion in Optimal Relationships." In C. R. Knee & H. T. Reis (Eds.), *Positive Approaches to Optimal Relationship Development*. Cambridge, UK: Cambridge University Press, pp. 171-196.

[359] Vallerand, R. J., (2015), *op. cit.*, p. 11.

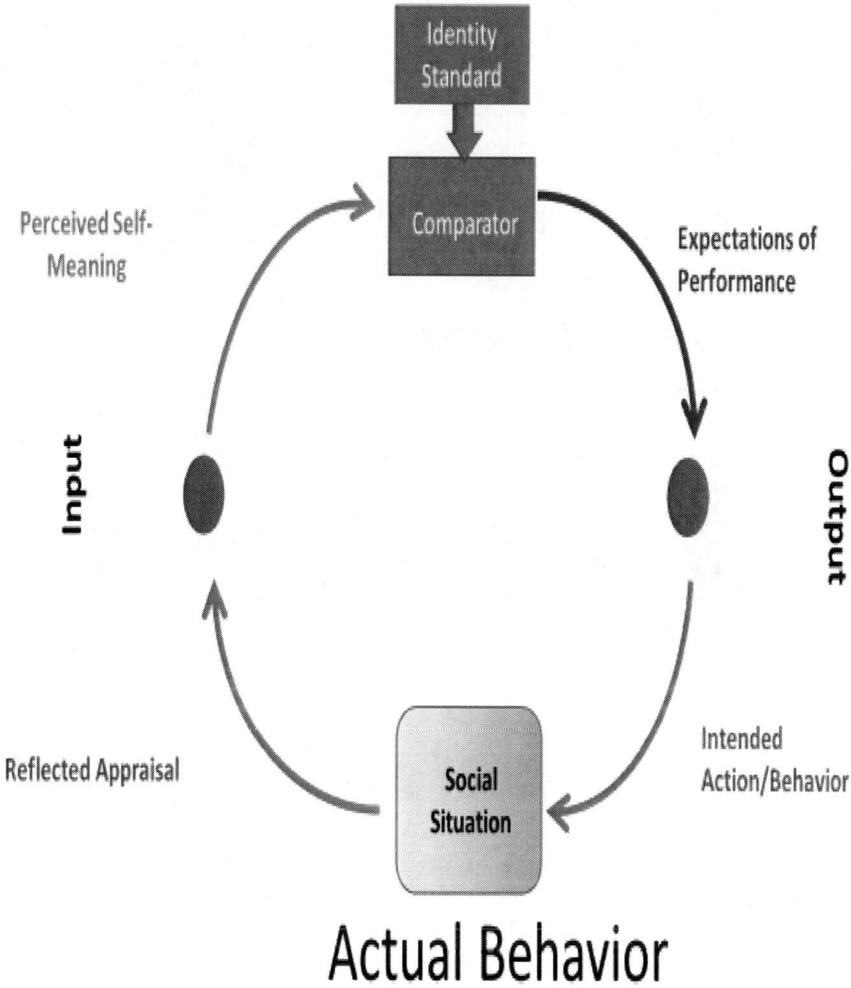

Figure 1. The Identity Standard.

Peter Burke and Jan Stets have provided a model which represents how individuals consciously and subconsciously make decisions associated with their perceptions about who they are and the values that guide them. The identity standard or comparator in this model reflects the values and responsibilities which each individual establishes as the criteria by which (s)he chooses to guide her/his personal choices and interactions with others.

As individuals assess their own actions and receive feedback from others, they then compare their actual conduct with the criteria from their original identity standard/comparator and choose to either amend that standard or increase their effort to conform with its criteria.

Those criteria are subjectively translated into specific interpersonal actions and behaviors, but those behavioral standards evolve as persons interact with others based upon the context of situations. As individuals assess their own actions and receive feedback from others, they then compare their actual conduct with the criteria from their original identity standard/comparator and choose to either amend that standard or increase their effort to conform with its criteria. Table 1 summarizes the eight elements of the identity process and explains the identity standard and how leaders make conscious or subconscious decisions about their behaviors.

Table 1. Explanation of the identity process

Identity Element	Description	Moral Component	Comment
Comparator	The comparator is a set of general ideals by which a person defines his/her own standards for guiding personal conduct.	These standards typically incorporate moral variables about duties, rules, relationships, and responsibilities.	Moral identity incorporates this comparator as a generalized definition of beliefs and values.

Identity Element	Description	Moral Component	Comment
Expectations of Performance	Expectations of performance translate the general ideals into more specific guidelines for actions and personal conduct	Expectations are generalized but are nonetheless moral and ethical, principle-centered, and values-based	These expectations translate general ideals into much more specific guidelines for individual conduct
Output	The output constitutes specific criteria about one's identity and what a person believes is his/her specific obligations associated with her/his conduct	Outputs are, once again, morally and ethically important identifiers that equate with how one ought to act.	Outputs are the metrics by which a person evaluates his or her ideal standards and conduct. This output measure establishes criteria for one's future actions
Intended Actions or Behavior	The output is equated to specific actions and behaviors that demonstrate a person's commitment to beliefs and values	Actions or behaviors are anticipated responses that are duty-based but often situation-dependent as well	Intended actions and behaviors are the means whereby standards are equated to conduct but intentions can also be affected by context
Social Situation	The social situation is the specific context in which a person actually interacts with others and includes her/his capacity to act in that situation	The social situation and its accompanying pressures directly influence individual choices and may result in a failure to honor moral responsibilities.	Unanticipated situations, limited resources, time pressure, and social influences can have a major impact on personal choices and make "desired" responses difficult.
Reflected Appraisal	Reflected appraisal includes feedback from others but also is made up of one's view of his or her actions, compared to his/her intentions	The reflected appraisal can result in guilt about actions or can reinforce positive intentions actually carried out	This reflected appraisal provides the opportunity to assess one's conduct, based upon a situation
Input	Input is the value-based self-assessment that results from one's personal choices and affirms or disconfirms one's identity	Input becomes a moral and ethical self-assessment according to the criteria of the comparator.	This assessment of value is a positive or negative data point for evaluating personal conduct
Perceived Self-Meaning	The perceived self-meaning is the inference that a person draws about her/his ability to conform conduct to the identity standard	The perceived self-meaning can reinforce values or cause a person to reevaluate her/his future comparator	Rationalizing can occur to protect one's self-esteem or can inspire a person to make a greater effort

Relating the identity to the passion that individuals incorporate in their lives, the choices and responses of passion to circumstances, goals, and events align with their individual identities. How a person chooses to respond is a function of the strength of their identity standard or comparator and whether they accurately perceive the implications of their actions that are associated with desired outcomes[360]. Individuals that persist in making passion-driven choices that are dysfunctional, excessively stress producing, and/or inconsistent with achieving their desires must either modify how they respond or find themselves in the position where their passion becomes a negative force in their lives[361].

How a person chooses to respond is a function of the strength of their identity standard or comparator and whether they accurately perceive the implications of their actions that are associated with desired outcomes.

Self-awareness about the consequences of individual choices can enable individuals to modify an obsessive and dysfunctional passionate response. The self-control that enables a person to choose to direct their passion along a more harmonious and constructive path can enable individuals to be more successful as they pursue a desired objective or engage in an activity or pattern of behavior. By understanding and applying the insights that come from self-knowledge and self-awareness, the identity standard becomes the vehicle by which individuals can more effectively govern their passions with self-control[362].

---

360 Caldwell, C., (2020). "Acquiring Meaning through Self-Understanding." *Communication, Meaning, and Identity: Moving Toward Discovery*. Hauppauge, NY: NOVA Publishing, Chapter 6.

361 Vallerand, R. J., (2015), *op. cit.*

362 *Ibid.*

By understanding and applying the insights that come from self-knowledge and self-awareness, the identity standard becomes the vehicle by which individuals can more effectively govern their passions with self-control.

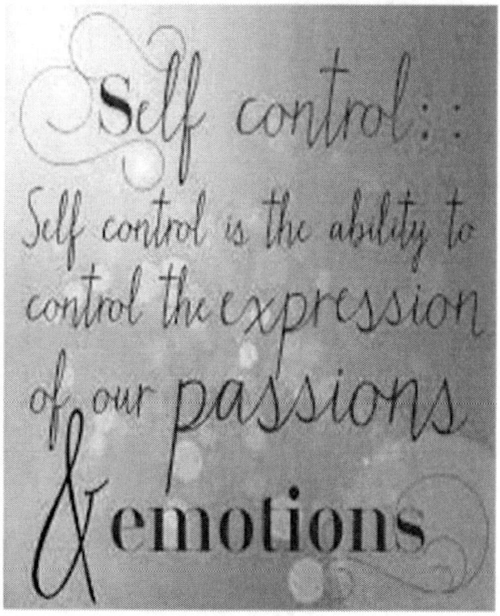

Suggestions for Leaders

As leaders contemplate how they can most effectively incorporate insights about passion as they establish relationships with others, their understanding of the identity standard can help them to increase their effectiveness in creating those relationships. We offer six specific suggesions for assisting leaders as they integrate their passion and identity in serving others.

1) Recruit and Retain Colleagues Who Share a Passionate Commitment to a Common Purpose

Hiring and retaining employees who share a passionate commitment to a common purpose increases the ability of an organization to excel and enhances a leader's effectiveness[363]. Sharing a passion, purpose, and sense of mission with employees unites an organization in the pursuit of a common set of

---

[363] Collins, J., (2001). *Good to Great: Why Some Companies Make the Leap. . . And Others Don't*. New York: Harper Collins.

objectives[364]. Leaders with passion, or a fierce resolve to fulfill the best possible outcomes of an organization, who combine that commitment with integrity and humility are able to earn the trust and followership of employees[365].

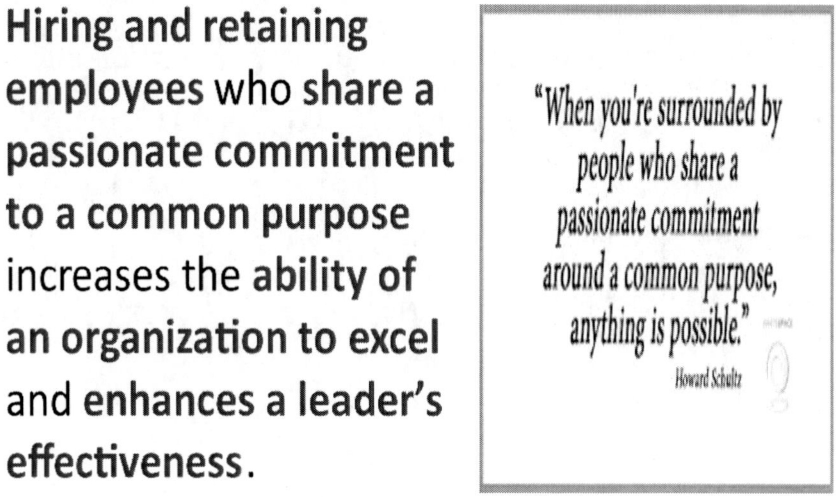

2) Identify and Abide by Positive Values and Principles Aligned with a Worthy Purpose

Employees are more committed and organizations are more successful when employees' values and principles are aligned in the pursuit of a meaningful outcome[366]. These same companies who focus on a valued purpose have also proven to be more profitable than companies that establish as their objective the maximization of profits[367]. Employees of those companies are more dedicated and focused and buy in to the company's commitment to high ideals and outcomes that benefit society[368].

---

364 Barnard, C. I., (1938). *The Functions of the Executive*. Cambridge, MA: Harvard College.

365 Collins, J., (2001). *Good to Great: Why Some Companies Make the Leap. . . And Others Don't*. New York: Harper Collins.

366 Collins, J. & Porras, J. I, (2004). *Built to Last: Successful Habits of Visionary Companies*. New York: Harper Collins.

367 *Ibid*.

368 *Ibid*.

Employees are more committed and organizations are more successful when employees' values and principles are aligned in the pursuit of a meaningful outcome.

3) Maintain Standards of Personal Behavior that Comply with Those Values and Principles

Leaders whose actions match the values that they advocate for their companies are viewed by employees as more credible and trustworthy than leaders whose behaviors do not match their companies' declared values[369]. Employees who work for those same leaders are also much more likely to match their level of personal commitment and passion as well[370].

Leaders whose actions match the values that they advocate for their companies are viewed by employees as more credible and trustworthy than leaders whose behaviors do not match their companies' declared values.

[369] Schein, E. H. & Schein, P. A., (2016). *Organizational Culture and Leadership* (5th ed.). San Francisco, CA: Jossey-Bass.
[370] *Ibid.*

4) Regularly Monitor Actions to Ensure that They Match Values and Principles

Leaders who adopt Identity Theory's regular assessment of their actions and behaviors and who make that assessment based upon their identity standard criteria's values and principles are more likely to not only increase their personal commitment to their identity but also will be more successful at earning the trust of others[371]. Their commitment to those values and principles is also aligned with their personal passion to excel and to become their best version of themselves[372].

5) Acknowledge When Passion-Driven Behaviors Conflict with a Balanced Life

A commitment to excel and to be extraordinary is a fundamental criterion of passion-driven behavior[373]. When those behaviors are out of balance with other important life priorities those behaviors need to be acknowledged and carefully reconsidered. Closely monitoring personal choices, identifying when those choices conflict with the identity standard, and recognizing when actions demonstrate obsessive passion-driven behaviors can be a powerful way of identifying the alignment of those behaviors with core principles and values[374].

---

[371] Burke, P. J. & Stets, J. E., (2009), *op. cit.*
[372] Covey, S. R., (1992). *Principle-Centered Leadership*. New York: Touchstone Books.
[373] Vallerand, R. J., (2015), *op. cit.*
[374] Burke, P. J. & Stets, J. E., (2009), *op. cit.*

A commitment to excel and to be extraordinary is a fundamental criterion of passion-driven behavior. When behavioral choices are out of balance with other important life priorities those behaviors need to be acknowledged and carefully reconsidered.

6) Amend Dysfunctional and Unproductive Actions that Reflect Obsessive Passion

Formalizing the review of behaviors and applying the identity standard is an excellent way of identifying when actions are inconsistent with that standard. Identifying whether choices are obsessive, dysfunctional, anxiety producing, and unproductive can be a healthy way of modifying choices that are out of harmony with an individual's best interests. Better choices that are healthier and more uplifting can make a leader's life more satisfying but can also enable that leader to be more effective in working with others[375].

Identifying whether choices are obsessive, dysfunctional, anxiety producing, and unproductive can be a healthy way of modifying choices that are out of harmony with an individual's best interests

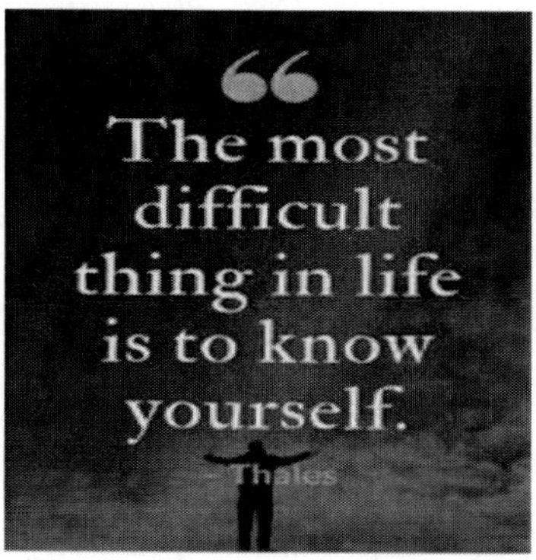

375 Vallerand, R. J. & Carbonneau, N., (2016), *op. cit.*

Each of these identity-related suggestions not only can help leaders to be more effective in their interpersonal relationships and organizational roles but can assist them to be able to combine their passion with greater self-control[376]. The benefit for leaders is not only greater personal control of their choices and actions but an increased ability to make decisions that strengthen their organizations and improve their ability to lead.

The benefit for leaders is not only **greater personal control** of their **choices and actions** but an **increased ability to make decisions** that **strengthen their organizations** and **improve their ability to lead**.

Our Challenge

Leading with passion and self-control makes good sense–but acquiring the ability to management oneself and govern one's passions demands thoughtful self-awareness and a commitment to high values and true principles[377]. As leaders understand the nature of passion and can distinguish between obsessive and harmonious passion in their own lives, they are able to be more effective and psychologically healthier. Those qualities enable such leaders to increase their credibility and their ability to be perceived as trustworthy[378].

---

[376] Vallerand, R. J., (2015), *op. cit.*

[377] *Ibid.*

[378] Kouzes, J. M. & Posner, B. Z., (2011). *Credibility: How Leaders Gain and Lose It – Why People Demand It*. San Francisco, CA: Jossey-Bass.

As leaders understand the nature of passion and can distinguish between obsessive and harmonious passion in their own lives, they are able to be more effective and psychologically healthier.

We challenge leaders to examine the nature of their personal passions and thoughtfully assess the degree to which they may need to reevaluate their own choices and interactions. By thoughtfully reflecting on the degree to which their actions align with the values and principles of their identity standards, leaders will strengthen their ability to lead with integrity and consistency.

By thoughtfully reflecting on the degree to which their actions align with the values and principles of their identity standards, leaders will strengthen their ability to lead with integrity and consistency.

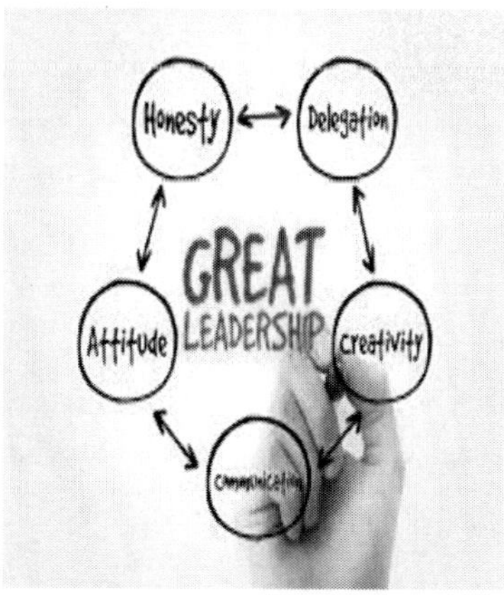

As leaders adopt the six suggestions for incorporating the identity standard with their own choices as they seek to motivate and guide those with whom they work, harmonious passion can be a powerful resource when combined with thoughtful self-assessment and self-control. Aligning healthy passions with the best interests of a leader's organization and those whom (s)he leads is the essence of self-control and effective leadership.

References

Barnard, C. I., (1938). *The Functions of the Executive*. Cambridge, MA: Harvard College.

Burke, P. J. & Stets, J. E., (2009). *Identity Theory*. Oxford, UK: Oxford University Press.

Caldwell, C., (2020). "Acquiring Meaning through Self-Understanding." *Communication, Meaning, and Identity: Moving Toward Discovery*. Hauppauge, NY: NOVA Publishing, Chapter 6.

Collins, J., (2001). *Good to Great: Why Some Companies Make the Leap. . .And Others Don't*. New York: Harper Collins.

Collins, J. & Porras, J. I, (2004). *Built to Last: Successful Habits of Visionary Companies*. New York: Harper Collins.

Covey, S. R., (1992). *Principle-Centered Leadership*. New York: Touchstone Books.

Kouzes, J. M. & Posner, B. Z., (2011). *Credibility: How Leaders Gain and Lose It – Why People Demand It*. San Francisco, CA: Jossey-Bass.

Schein, E. H. & Schein, P. A., (2016). *Organizational Culture and Leadership* (5th ed.). San Francisco, CA: Jossey-Bass.

Vallerand, R. J. & Carbonneau, N., (2016). "The Role of Passion in Optimal Relationships." In C. R. Knee & H. T. Reis (Eds.), *Positive Approaches to Optimal Relationship Development*. Cambridge, UK: Cambridge University Press, pp. 171-196.

Vallerand, R. J., (2015). *The Psychology of Passion: A Dualistic Model*. Oxford, UK: Oxford University Press.

Vallerand, R. J. Paquet, Y. Fillipe, F. L. & Charest, J., (2010). On the Role of Passion for Work in Burnout: A Process Model." *Journal of Personality*, Vol. 78, Iss. 1, pp. 289-312.

Vallerand, R. J. & Houlfort, N (2003). "Passion at Work: Toward a New Conceptualization." In S. W. Gilliland, D. D. Steiner & D. P. Skarlicki (Eds.). *Emerging Perspectives on Values in Organizations*. Greenwich, CN: Information Age Publishing, pp. 175-204.

Vallerand, R. J., Salvy, S.-J., Mageau, G. A., Elliot, A. J., Denis, P. L., Grouzet, F. M. E. & Blanchard, C., (2007). "On the Role of Passion in Performance." *Journal of Personality*, Vol. 75, Iss. 3, pp. 505-534.

References

"Stephen Covey Principles Quotes." LibQuotes.com. Found online on October 13, 2021 at Stephen Covey Quotes about Principles - Lib Quotes.

Amiel, H. F. & Ward, H., (2012). *Amiel's Journal*. Charleston, SC: BiblioLife Publishers.

Andersen, E. (2012). *Leading So People Will Follow*. San Francisco, CA: Jossey-Bass, p. 1.

Anderson, V. & Caldwell, C., (2019). "Transforming People: Creating a Culture of Change." In C. Caldwell & V. Anderson, *Human Resource Management: A Transformative Approach*. Hauppauge, NY: NOVA Publishing, Chapter 7.

Aquinas, T., (1956). *Scriptum super Sententiis*. Lethielleux-Rousteau, France: Lethielleux Publishers, SsS III, 26.

Aquinas, T., (2012). *Summa Theologiae Prima Pars. Dubuque, IA: Emmaus Academic,* ST II-II 17.6.

Atwijuka, S., & Caldwell, C., (2017). "Authentic Leadership and the Ethic of Care." *Journal of Management Development*, Vol. 36, Iss. 8, pp. 1040-

Aurelius, M., (2019). *Meditations*. New York: SDE Book Publishers, Book 5.

Bandura, A. (1977). "Self-Efficacy: Toward a Unifying Theory of Behavioral Change." *Psychological Review*, Vol. 84, pp. 191-215.

Barnard, C. I., (1938). *The Functions of the Executive*. Cambridge, MA: Harvard College.

Bauman, D. C., (2013). "Leadership and the Three Face of Integrity." *The Leadership Quarterly*, Vol. 24, Iss. 3, pp. 414-426.

Bayer, R. C., Davis, J. H. & Schoorman, F. D., (1995). "An Integrative Model of Organizational Trust." *Academy of Management Review*, Vol. 20, No. 3, pp. 709-734.

Becker, E. F. & Wortmann, J., (2009). *Mastering Communication at Work: How to Lead, Manage, and Influence*. Boston, MA: McGraw-Hill Education.

Beer, M., (2009). *High Commitment High Performance: How to Build a Resilient Organization for Sustained Advantage*. San Francisco, CA: Jossey-Bass.

Blanchard, K., (1990). *Democrat and Chronicle* cited in Shakohl, T., (2019). "Fact Check: Did C. S. Lewis Say, 'Humility Isn't Thinking Less of Yourself – It's Thinking of Yourself Less'?" found online on October 8, 2021 at FACT CHECK: Did CS Lewis Say, 'Humility Isn't Thinking Less Of Yourself – It's Thinking Of Yourself Less'? | Check Your Fact.

Block, P., (2013). *Stewardship: Choosing Service Over Self-Interest*. San Francisco: Jossey-Bass.

Bloeser, C. & Stahl, T., (2017). "Hope." In E. N. Zalta, (Ed.). The Stanford Encyclopedia of Philosophy. Found online on October 14, 2021 at Author and Citation Information for "Hope" (stanford.edu).

Bock, C., (2016). "Hope in Ancient Greece: Aristotle on Hope, Optimism, and Courage." April 25, 2016 and found online on October 14, 2021 at Hope in Ancient Greek: Aristotle on hope, optimism, and courage – Cherice Bock,

Browning, R. M., (2005). *Resolving Concerns*. Atlanta, GA: Self-published.

Bruneau, M., (2016). "These 7 Qualities Lead to Perseverance when Faced with Adversity." *Forbes*, September 26, 2016 and found online on October 10, 2021 at These 7 Qualities Lead To Perseverance When Faced With Adversity (forbes.com).

Burke, P. J. & Stets, J. E., (2009). *Identity Theory*. Oxford, UK: Oxford University Press.

Burns, J. M., (2010). *Leadership*. New York: Harper Perennial.

Caldwell, C. & Anderson, V. (2019). "Humility and Personal Progress: Insights about Identity" in Anderson, V. & Caldwell, C., (Eds.), *Humility as Enlightened Leadership*. Hauppauge, NY: NOVA Publishers, Chapter 3.

Caldwell, C. & Anderson, V., (2019). "Elements of Humility: A Virtuous Perspective." In Anderson, V. & Caldwell, C., (Eds.) *Humility as Enlightened Leadership*. Hauppauge, NY: NOVA Publishing, Chapter 2.

Caldwell, C. & Anderson, V., (2019). "Love: The Heart of Leadership – Introduction and Overview" in C. Caldwell & V. Anderson (Eds.), *Leading with Love*. Hauppauge, NY: NOVA Publishers, Chapter 1.

Caldwell, C. & Anderson, V., (2019). "Love: The Heart of Leadership, Introduction and Overview." In C. Caldwell & V. Anderson, (Eds.), *Leading with Love*. Hauppauge, NY: NOVA Publishing.

Caldwell, C. & Anderson, V., (2019). "Stewardship as a Transformative Model." In C. Caldwell & V. Anderson (Eds.), *Trust, Trustworthiness, and Stewardship: A Transformative Approach*. Hauppauge, New York: NOVA Publishing, Chapter 5.

Caldwell, C. & Anderson, V., (2019). "Trust from a Transformative Perspective" in *Trust, Trustworthiness, and Stewardship: A Transformative Approach*. C. Caldwell & V. Anderson (Eds.) .Hauppauge, New York: NOVA Publishing, Chapter 3.

Caldwell, C. & Anderson, V., (2021). "Moral Identity and Finding Your Voice" in C. Caldwell & V. Anderson (Eds.). *Moral Identity and Self-Discovery*. Hauppauge, NY: NOVA Publishers, Chapter 2.

Caldwell, C. & Anderson, V., (2021). "Moral Identity in an Uncertain World." In C. Caldwell & V. Anderson (Eds.), *Moral Identity and Self-Discovery*. Hauppauge, NY: NOVA Publishing, Chapter 1.

Caldwell, C. & Anderson, V., (2021). "Moral Identity, Self-Improvement, and the Quest for Greatness: A Leadership Responsibility." *Journal of Values-Based Leadership*, Vol. 14, Iss. 2, Article 4 found online at Moral Identity, Self-Improvement, and the Quest for Greatness: A Leadership Responsibility (valpo.edu).

Caldwell, C. & Anderson, V., (Eds.) (2019). "Love and Trust: The Leader's Gifts" in *Leading with Love*, C. Caldwell, C. & V. Anderson, V., (Eds.): Hauppauge, New York: NOVA Publishing, Chapter 10.

Caldwell, C. & Anderson, V., (Eds.). (2019). "Stewardship as a Transformative Model." In C. Caldwell & V. Anderson (Eds.) *Trust, Trustworthiness, and Stewardship: A Transformative Approach*. Hauppauge, New York: NOVA Publishing, Chapter 5.

Caldwell, C., (2012). *Moral Leadership: A Transformative Model for Tomorrow's Leaders*. New York: Business Expert Press.

Caldwell, C., (2020). "Acquiring Meaning through Self-Understanding." *Communication, Meaning, and Identity: Moving Toward Discovery*. Hauppauge, NY: NOVA Publishing, Chapter 6.

Caldwell, C., (2020). "Acquiring Meaning through Self-Understanding." *Communication, Meaning, and Identity: Moving Toward Discovery*. Hauppauge, NY: NOVA Publishing, Chapter 6.

Caldwell, C., and Ndalamba, K. K., (2017). "Trust and Being 'Worthy' – The Keys to Creating Wealth." *Journal of Management Development*, Vol. 36, Iss. 8, pp. 1076-1086.

Caldwell, C., Davis, B., and Devine, J. A., (2009). "Trust, Faith, and Betrayal: Insights from Management for the Wise Believer." *Journal of Business Ethics*, Vol. 89, Iss. 1, pp. 103-114.

Caldwell, C., Floyd, L. A., Taylor, J. & Woodard, B. (2014). "Beneficence as a Source of Competitive Advantage." *Journal of Management Development*, Vol. 33, Iss. 10, pp. 1057-1069.

Caldwell, C., Hayes, L., Karri, R., & Bernal, P., (2008). "Ethical Stewardship: Implications for Leadership and Trust." *Journal of Business Ethics*, Vol. 78, Iss. 1/2, pp. 153-164.

Caldwell, C., Truong, D., Linh, P., and Tuan, A., (2011). "Strategic Human Resource Management as Ethical Stewardship." *Journal of Business Ethics*, Vol. 98, Iss. 1., pp. 171-182.

Carver, C. S., & Scheier, M. F. (1999). "Optimism." In C. R. Snyder (Ed.), *Coping, The Psychology of What Works*, NY: Oxford University Press, pp. 182-204.

Carver, C.S. (1979). "A Cybernetic Model of Self-Attention Processes." *Journal of Personality and Social Psychology*, Vol. 37, pp. 1251-1281.

Castillo, B. (2008). *Self-Coaching 101: Use Your Mind – Don't Let It Use You*. Fayetteville, NC: Futures Unlimited Coaching.

Cherry, H., (2021). "What is Humility?" Charles Koch Institute. August 4, 2021 and found online on October 8, 2021 at What is humility? - Charles Koch Institute.

Christensen, C. M., (2016). *The Innovator's Dilemma: When New Technologies Cause Great Firms to Fail*. Boston, MA: Harvard Business Review Press.

Christensen, C. M., Allworth, J. & Dillon, K., (2012). *How Will You Measure Your Life?* New York: Harper Business.

Clifton, J. & Harter, J., (2019). *It's the Manager*. Omaha, NE: Gallup Press.

Clifton, J., (2021). "Gallup Finds a Silver Bullet: Coach Me Once Per Week." Gallup, May 27, 2021 and found online on July 11, 2021 at Gallup Finds a Silver Bullet: Coach Me Once Per Week.

Collins, J., (2001). "Level 5 Leadership: The Triumph of Humility and Fierce Resolve." *Harvard Business Review*, January 1, 2001 and found online on October 5, 2001 at Level 5 Leadership: The Triumph of Humility and Fierce Resolve (hbr.org).

Collins, J. & Hansen, M. T., (2011). *Great by Choice: Uncertainty, Chaos, and Luck—Why Some Thrive Despite Them All*. New York: HarperCollins.

Collins, J. & Porras, J. I., (2004). *Built to Last: Successful Habits of Visionary Companies*. New York: HarperCollins.

Collins, J., (2001). *Good to Great: Why Some Companies Make the Leap. . . And Others Don't*. New York: HarperCollins.

Covey, S. R. (2004). *The 8th Habit: From Effectiveness to Greatness*. New York: Free Press.

Covey, S. R., (1992). *Principle-Centered Leadership*. New York: Touchstone Printing.

Davenport, B., (2017). “How Seeking Your Passion Boosts Self-Esteem.” Huff Post, December 6, 2017 and found online on May 15, 2021 at How Seeking Your Passion Boosts Self-Esteem | HuffPost Life.

Davis, J. H., Schoorman, F. D. & Donaldson, L., (1997). “Toward a Stewardship Theory of Management.” *Academy of Management Review*, Vol. 22, No. 1, pp. 20–47.

Deming, W. E., (2000). *Out of the Crisis*. Cambridge, MA: MIT Press.

DePree, M., (2004). *Leadership is an Art*. New York: Crown Publishers and Covey, S. R., (2004). *The 8th Habit: From Effectiveness to Greatness*. New York: Free Press.

Descartes, R. & Moriarty, M., (2016) *The Passions of the Soul and Other Late Philosophical Writings*. Oxford, UK: Oxford University Press.

Duckworth, A., (2018). *GRIT: The Power of Passion and Persistence*. London, UK: Vermilion Publishing.

Duckworth, A.L., Peterson, C., Matthews, M.D., & Kelly, D.R. (2007). “Grit: Perseverance and Passion for Long-term Goals.” *Journal of Personality and Social Psychology*, Vol. 92, pp. 1087- 1101.

Edelman, (2021). “Edelman Trust Barometer 2021.” Found online on July 4, 2021 at 2021 Edelman Trust Barometer | Edelman.

Ellinger, A. D. Ellinger, A., Hamlin, R. G. & Beattie, R. S., (2009). “Achieving Improved Performance through Managerial Coaching.” In R. Watkins & D. Leigh (Eds.). *Handbook of Improving Performance in the Workplace*, Vol. 2: Selecting and Implementing Performance Interventions., San Francisco, CA: Jossey-Bass, pp. 275-298.

Elmore, R. (2008), "Leadership as the Practice of Improvement." In Hopkins, D., D. Nusche & B. Pont (Eds.), *Improving School Leadership, Volume 2: Case Studies on System Leadership*. Paris, France: OECD Publishing.

Fishbein, M & Ajzen, I., (2011). *Predicting and Changing Behavior: The Reasoned Action Approach*. East Sussex, UK: Psychology Press.

Fitz-Enz, J., (2009). *The ROI of Human Capital: Measuring the Economic Value of Employee Performance*. New York: AMACOM.

Follett, M. P., (2013). *Dynamic Administration: The Collected Papers of Mary Parker Follett*. Eastford, CT: Martino Fine Books.

Forman, C. & Ungard, B., (2019). *The Practice of Self-Management: A Handbook for Walking the Path from Reactivity to Presence and Connection*. Austin, TX: Conscious Capitalism Press.

Frankl, V. E., (2006). *Man's Search for Meaning*. Boston, MA: Beacon Press.

Frankl, V., (1988). *Man's Search for Meaning*. New York: Pocket Books.

Frick, Don M. (2004). *Robert K. Greenleaf: A Life of Servant Leadership*. San Francisco: Berrett-Koehler Publishers.

Fromm, E., (2006). *The Art of Loving*. New York: Harper Perennial.

George, B., (2004). *Authentic Leadership: Rediscovering the Secrets to Creating Lasting Value*. San Francisco, CA: Jossey-Bass.

Gillespie, P., (2016). “America's Part-time Work Force Is Huge.” CNN Business, April 25, 2016 and found online on July 9, 2021 at America's part-time problem may be permanent (cnn.com).

Gilligan, C., (2016). *In a Different Voice: Psychological Theory and Women's Development*. Boston, MA: Harvard University Press.

Glauber, R. K., (2013). "Wanting More but Working Less: Involuntary Part-time Employment and Economic Vulnerability." Carsey Institute, University of New Hampshire. Found online on July 9, 2021 at "Wanting more but working less: involuntary part-time employment and ec" by Rebecca K. Glauber (unh.edu).

Goleman, D., (2005). *Emotional Intelligence: Why It Can Matter More Than IQ*. New York: Bantam Publishing.

Greene, R. J., (2018). *Rewarding Performance: Guiding Principles; Custom Strategies* (2nd ed.). London, UK: Routledge.

Greenleaf, R. K., (1996). "The Requirements of Responsibility." In D. M. Frick & L. C. Spears (Eds.), *On Becoming a Servant Leader*. San Francisco, CA: Jossey-Bass, pp. 41-52.

Greenleaf, R. K., (2002). *Servant Leadership: A Journey into the Nature of Legitimate Power and Greatness 25th Anniversary Edition*. Mahwah, NJ: Paulist Press.

Greenleaf, R. K., (2015). *The Servant as Leader*. Indianapolis, IN: The Greenleaf Center for Servant Leadership, p. 2.

Greenleaf, R.K., (2007). "The Servant as Leader." In W. C. Zimmerli, K. Richter & M. Holzinger, (Eds.) *Corporate Ethics and Corporate Governance*. New York: Springer, pp. 79–85

Greerson, R. R., (1962). "On Enthusiasm." *Journal of the American Psychological Association*, Vol. 10, pp. 3-21.

Hackman J. R, & Oldham, G. R., (1976). "Motivation through the Design of Work: Test of a Theory." *Organizational Behavior and Human Performance,* Vol. 16, pp. 250-279.

Harrington, M., (2017). Survey: People's Trust has Declined in Business, Media, Government, and NGOs." *Harvard Business Review*, January 16, 2017 and found online on May 13, 2021 at https://hbr.org/2017/01/survey-peoples-trust-has-declined-in-business-media-government-and-ngo.

Helland, M. R., & Winston, B. E., (2005). "Toward a Deeper Understanding of Hope and Leadership." *Journal of Leadership and Organizational Studies*, Vol. 12, No. 2, pp. 42-54.

Hellebuyck, M., Nguyen, T. Halphern, M., Fritze, D. & Kennedy, J., (2017). *Mind the Workplace*. Lancaster, CA: Mental Health America.

Ho, L. (2020). "How to Connect Passion and Purpose for Fulfillment in Life." Lifehack, July 17, 2020 and found online on May 15, 2021 at How To Connect Passion and Purpose For Fulfillment In Life (lifehack.org).

Hobbes, T. & Schneider, H. W., (2017). *Leviathan*. Boston, MA: Digireads.com Publishing, Chapter LVI.14.

Hosmer. L. T., (2010). *The Ethics of Management* (7th Ed.). Boston, MA: McGraw-Hill Education.

Hughes, C., (2012). *Valuing People and Technology in the Workplace: A Competitive Advantage Framework*. Hershey, PA: IGI Global.

Hume, David, [1738] (2007). *A Treatise of Human Nature*. In D. F. Norton and M. J. Norton (Eds.). Oxford. UK Oxford University Press.

Investing.com, (2016). "Nearly 95% of All New Jobs During Obama Era Were Part-time, or Contract." Found online on July 9, 2021 at Nearly 95% of all new jobs during Obama era were part-time, or contract By Investing.com.

James Kouzes. "20 Servant Leadership Quotes that Elevate Our Thinking." *RickConlow.com.* Found online on October 13, 2021 at 20 Servant Leadership Quotes that Elevate our Thinking - Rick Conlow.

James, W., (2015). *The Will to Believe and Other Essays in Popular Philosophy*: New York: Dover Publications.

John Quincy Adams Quotes (Leadership). GraciousQuotes,com. Found online on October 13, 2021 at 30 John Quincy Adams Quotes (LEADERSHIP) (graciousquotes.com).

Johnson, D., Citera, M. & Wrench, J. S., (2014). *Training and Development: The Intersection of Communication and Talent Development in the Modern Workplace.* Dubuque, IA: Kendall Hunt Publishing.

Josephson, M., (2016). "Commentary: Intellectual Humility and the Pursuit of Wisdom. 'Don't Believe Everything You Think.'" *Whatwillmatter.com* found online on October 8, 2021 at Commentary: INTELLECTUAL HUMILITY AND THE PURSUIT OF WISDOM. "Don't believe everything you think." | What Will Matter.

Katz, L. F. & Krueger, A. B., (2018). "The Rise and Nature of Work Arrangements in the United States, 1995-2015." *Industrial and Labor Relations Review*, Vol. 72, Iss. 2, pp. 382-416.

King, M. & Carruthers, P., (2012). "Moral Responsibility and Consciousness." *Journal of Moral Philosophy*, Vol. 9, pp. 200-228.

Kleckner, J., (2018). "80 Albert Einstein Quotes to Inspire You for Life." Addicted2Success, December 18, 2018 and found online on October 10, 2021 at 80 Albert Einstein Quotes to Inspire You For Life (addicted2success.com).

Kouzes, J. M. & Posner, B. Z. (2011). *Credibility: How Leaders Gain and Lose It, Why People Demand It.* San Francisco, CA: Jossey-Bass.

Kouzes, J. M. & Posner, B. Z., (2003). *Encouraging the Heart: A Leader's Guide to Rewarding and Recognizing Others*. San Francisco, CA: Jossey-Bass.

Kouzes, J. M. & Posner, B.Z., (2017). *The Leadership Challenge: How to Make Extraordinary Things Happen in Organizations* (7th ed.). San Francisco, CA: Jossey-Bass, pp. 93-142.

Kupperman, J., (1995). *Character*. Oxford, UK: Oxford University Press.

LeBlanc, L., Sellers, T. & Ala'I, S., (2020). *Building and Sustaining Meaningful and Effective Relationships as a Supervisor and Mentor*. Hudson, NY: Sloan Educational Publishing.

Lee, C., (2020). *Performance Conversations: How to Use Questions to Coach Employees, Improve Productivity, and Boost Confidence (Without Appraisals).* Alexandria, VA: Society for Human Resource Management.

Ludema, J. D., Wilmot, T. B., & Srivastva, S., (1997). "Organization Hope: Reaffirming the Constructive Task of Social and Organizational Inquiry." *Human Relations*, Vol. 50, No. 8, pp. 1015-1053.

Lufi, D. & Cohen, A., (1987). "A Scale for Measuring Persistence in Children." *Journal of Personality Assessment*, Vol. 51, No. 2, pp. 178-185.

Luthans, K, (2000). "Recognition: A Powerful, but often Overlooked, Leadership Tool to Improve Employee Performance." *Journal of Leadership and Organizational Studies*, Vol. 7, Iss. 1, pp. 31-39Mayer, R. C., Davis, J. H., & Schoorman, F. D., (1995). "An Integrative Model of Organizational Trust." *Academy of Management Review*. Vol 20, No. 3, pp. 709-734.

Maholmes, V., (2014). *Fostering Resilience and Well-Being in Children and Families in Poverty: Why Hope Still Matters*. Oxford, UK: Oxford University Press.

Marian Anderson. "20 Servant Leadership Quotes that Elevate Our Thinking." *RickConlow.com*. Found online on October 13, 2021 at 20 Servant Leadership Quotes that Elevate our Thinking - Rick Conlow.

Maslow, A. H., (1993). *The Farther Reaches of Human Nature*. New York: Penguin/Arkana.

Maslow, A. H., (1994). *Religions, Values, and Peak-Experiences*. New York: Penguin Books.

Maudlin, J., (2021). "4 Economic Challenges for 2021." *Forbes*, January 18, 2021 and found online on July 4, 2021 at 4 Economic Challenges For 2021 (forbes.com).

Maxwell, Nan L. 2006. "Low-SkilCed Jobs: The Reality Behind the Popular Perceptions." In *The Working Life: The Labor Market for Workers in Low-Skilled Jobs*. Kalamazoo, MI: W.E. Upjohn Institute for Employment Research, pp. 1-23.

Mayer, R. C., Davis, J. H. & Schoorman, F. D., (1995). "An Integrative Model of Organizational Trust." *Academy of Management Review*, Vol. 20, No. 3, pp. 709-734.

Meier, G. & Albrecht. M. H., (2003). "The Persistence Process: Development of a Stage Model for Goal-Directed Behavior." *Journal of Leadership and Organizational Studies*, Vol. 10, No. 2, pp. 43-54.

Meirav, A., (2009). "The Nature of Hope." *Ratio: An International Journal of Analytic Philosophy*. Vol. 22, Iss. 2, pp. 216-233.

Merriam-Webster Online Dictionary. "Enthusiasm." Found online on October 17, 2021 at Enthusiasm | Definition of Enthusiasm by Merriam-Webster.

Mirsirlisoy, E. (2018). "It's Not All Perseverance, You Need Passion Too." December 8, 2018 and found online on May 15, 2021 at Grit? It's Not All Perseverance, You Need Passion Too | by Erman Misirlisoy, PhD | Medium.

Murphy, J. J., (2010). *Leading with Passion: 10 Essentials for Inspiring Others*. Naperville, IL: Simple Truths Publishing.

Murray, J., (2020). "What is an Arms Length Transaction?" *the balance small business*, October 30, 2020 and found online on July 5, 2021 at An Arm's Length Transaction: What Is It? (thebalancesmb.com).

Neck, C. P., Manz, C. C. & Houghton, J. D., (2019). *Self-Leadership: The Definitive Guide to Personal* Excellence (2nd ed.). Newbury Park, CA: SAGE Publishing.

Nelson Mandela Quotes. (n.d.). BrainyQuote.com. Found on May 13, 2021at https://www.brainyquote.com/quotes/nelson_mandela_391070.

Okpala, C. O. & Caldwell, C. (2019). "Humility, Forgiveness, and Love: The Heart of Ethical Stewardship." *Journal of Values-Based Leadership*, Vol. 12 Summer 2019 and found online at https://scholar.valpo.edu/jvbl/vol12/iss2/10/.

Owens, B. P. & Hekman, D. R., (2012). "Modeling How to Grow: An Inductive Examination of Humble Leader Behaviors, Contingencies, and Outcomes." *Academy of Management Review*, Vol. 55, No. 4, pp. 787-818.

Owens, B. P. & Hekman, D. R., (2016). "How Does Leader Humility Affect Team Performance? Exploring the Mechanisms of Contagion and Collective Promotion Focus." *Academy of Management Journal*, Vol. 59, No. 3, pp. 787-818.

Owens, B. P., (2009). *Humility in Organizational Leadership*. Seattle, WA: University of Washington Press.

Oxford University Press, (2008). *The Oxford New Greek Dictionary: The Essential Resource Revised and Updated*. New York: Berkley Publishing.

Peale, N. V., (2003). *Enthusiasm Makes the Difference*. New York: Touchstone.

Pennock, S. F., (2020). "Resilience in Positive Psychology: Bouncing Back and Staying Strong." *Positive Psychology*, December 10, 2020 and found online on May 15, 2021 at Resilience in Positive Psychology: Bouncing Back & Staying Strong.

Pfeffer, J., (1998). *The Human Equation: Building Profits by Putting People First*. Boston, MA: Harvard Business Review Press.

Pulsifer, B., "75 Quotes on Integrity" found online on October 8, 2021 at 75 Quotes on Integrity | Inspiring Workspaces by BOS.

Quast, L, (2012). "When a Boss Takes Credit for Your Work." *Forbes*, July 9, 2012 and found online on October 8, 2021 at When A Boss Takes Credit For Your Work (forbes.com).

Rhein, N., (2021). "Why Hiring is So Difficult Right Now." *Detroit Today*, June 7, 2021 and found online on July 9, 2021 at Why Hiring Is So Difficult Right Now | WDET.

Rousseau, D. M., (1995). *Psychological Contracts in Organizations: Understanding Written and Unwritten Agreements*. Thousand Oaks, CA: Sage Publications.

Rubin, J., (2016). "Self Confidence and Finding Your Life Passion." Lost Highway Blues, July 15, 2016 and found online on May 15, 2021 at Self-confidence and Finding Your Life Passion (janerubinphd.com) Solomon, R. C., (2003). "Emotions, Thoughts, and Feelings: "What is a 'Cognitive Theory' of the Emotions and Does It Neglect Affectivity?" *Royal Institute of Philosophy Supplement*, Vol. 52, pp. 1-18.

Schaffner, A. K., (2021). "What is Humility? The Power of Humility with 5 Practical Exercises." *Positive Psychology*, April 15, 2021 and found online on October 4, 2021 at What is Humility? The Power Of Humility with 5 Practical Exercises (positivepsychology.com).

Schein, E. H. & Schein, P. A. (2016). *Organizational Culture and Leadership* (5th ed.). San Francisco, CA: Jossey-Bass.

Schein, E. H. & Schein, P. A., (2016). Organizational Culture and Leadership (6th ed.). San Francisco, CA: Jossey-Bass and Simpson & Cacioppe, (2001).

Schwantes, M. (2017). "Research: Why 70 Percent of Employees Aren't Working to Their Full Potential Comes Down to 1 Simple Reason." Inc., November 22, 2017 and found online on July 10, 2021 at Research: Why 70 Percent of Employees Aren't Working to Their Full Potential Comes Down to 1 Simple Reason | Inc.com.

Schwantes, M., (2018). "A New Study Reveals 70 Percent of Employees Say They Are Actively Looking for a New Job. Here's the Reason in Five Words." *Inc.*, Dec. 4, 2018 and found online on July 10, 2021 at A New Study Reveals 70 Percent of Workers

Say They Are Actively Looking for a New Job. Here's the Reason in 5 Words | Inc.com.

Seltzer, L. F., (2018). "7 Downsides of Hope." *Psychology Today*, July 25, 2018 and found online on October 15, 2021 at 7 Downsides of Hope | Psychology Today.

Senge, P. M., (2006). *The Fifth Discipline: The Art & Practice of the Learning Organization*. New York: Doubleday.

Simpson, S. & Cacioppe, R. (2001), "Unwritten Ground Rules: Transforming Organization Culture to Achieve Key Business Objectives and Outstanding Customer Service." *Leadership & Organization Development Journal*, Vol. 22 No. 8, pp. 394-401.

Sinek, S., (2011). *Start with Why: How Great Leaders Inspire Everyone to Take Action*. New York: Portfolio.

Sipe, J. W. & Frick, D. M., (2015). *Seven Pillars of Servant Leadership: Practicing the Wisdom of Leading by Serving; Revised and Expanded Edition*. Mahwah, NJ: Paulist Press.

Sjoberg, L. & Auden, W. H., (1965). *Dag Hammarskjold – Markings*. New York: Alfred A. Knopf Publishing.

Spinoza, B. & Elwes, R. H. M., (2021). *Ethics*, Chapter III, p. 18.

Spurgeon, C. H., (1856). "Pride and Humility." Delivered on August 17, 1856, New Park Street Chapel, Southwark, London, UK.

Stone, B. & Ukleja, M., (2009). *The Ethics Challenge: Strengthening Your Integrity in a Greedy World*. New York: Morgan James Publishing.

Sturt & Nordstrom, (2018). "10 Shocking Workplace Stats You Need to Know." Forbes, March 8, 2018 and found online on September 30, 2020 at https://www.forbes.com/sites/davidsturt/2018/03/08/10-shocking-workplace-stats-you-need-to-know/#2a90c892f3af.

Sylvester, B., (2019). "Fact Check: Did Aristotle Say 'We are what we repeatedly do?'" CheckYourFact, June 16, 2019 and found online on October 10, 2021 at FACT CHECK: Did Aristotle Say, 'We Are What We Repeatedly Do'? | Check Your Fact.

Vallerand, R. J. & Carbonneau, N., (2016). "The Role of Passion in Optimal Relationships." In C. R. Knee & H. T. Reis (Eds.), *Positive Approaches to Optimal Relationship Development*. Cambridge, UK: Cambridge University Press, pp. 171-196.

Vallerand, R. J. & Houlfort, N (2003). "Passion at Work: Toward a New Conceptualization." In S. W. Gilliland, D. D. Steiner & D. P. Skarlicki (Eds.). *Emerging Perspectives on Values in Organizations*. Greenwich, CN: Information Age Publishing, pp. 175-204.

Vallerand, R. J. Paquet, Y. Fillipe, F. L. & Charest, J., (2010). On the Role of Passion for Work in Burnout: A Process Model." *Journal of Personality*, Vol. 78, Iss. 1, pp. 289-312.

Vallerand, R. J., (2015). *The Psychology of Passion: A Dualistic Model*. Oxford, UK: Oxford University Press.

Vallerand, R. J., Salvy, S.-J., Mageau, G. A., Elliot, A. J., Denis, P. L., Grouzet, F. M. E. & Blanchard, C., (2007). "On the Role of Passion in Performance." *Journal of Personality*, Vol. 75, Iss. 3, pp. 505-534.

Van Lint, I., (2021). "Characteristics of Successful People." Enthusiasm found online on May 15, 2021at Enthusiasm is passion. Enthusiasm is living your dream. - Enthusiasm - Ineke Van Lint (enthousiasme.info).

Vroom, V. (1964). *Work and Motivation*. New York, NY: Wiley and Sons.

Winter, J., (2019). Self-Discipline: How to Build Mental Toughness and Focus to Achieve Your Goals. Audiobook found online on July 21, 2021 at Self-Discipline: How To Build Mental Toughness And Focus To Achieve Your Goals - Kindle edition by Winters, John. Self-Help Kindle eBooks @ Amazon.com.

About the Authors

Cam Caldwell, PhD

Business Professor (Retired)

Dr. Cam Caldwell received his PhD in Human Resources and Organization Behavior from Washington State University where he was a Thomas S. Foley Graduate Fellow. He holds the Senior Professional and Global Professional in Human Resources professional certifications. Prior to earning his PhD, he worked as a Human Resource Director, City Manager, and Management Consultant for more than twenty years. This is his twenty-fourth book and he has published more than 100 papers about a variety of management and leadership topics.

Email: cam.caldwell@gmail.com

Verl Anderson, PhD

Business Professor, Dixie State University,
St. George, Utah, USA

Dr. Verl Anderson obtained his doctorate degree in Business Administration from Arizona State University. He is currently a professor in Management and International Business at Dixie State University, St George, Utah. He has taught university courses as a visiting professor in New Zealand and four universities in China. He has published 34 articles in the past two years on leadership, ethics, China culture, kindness, strategic management, and social responsibility. His research interests include China culture and international cultures. He has traveled extensively, and annually takes groups on cultural/educational tours to China and New Zealand.

Email: verl@dixie.edu

Index